Different Facets of Education

ABOUT THE AUTHOR

PANNEER SELVAM is born in Salem - Valappady of Tamil Nadu. He started his career as school teacher in New Delhi in the year 1991. He joins as lecturer in DIET, perundurai of Erode in 2000. Bharathiyar University were gave the Philosophy in Doctorates in Language and Education. He is the seventh diploma holder from National University of Educational Planning and Administration (NUEPA), New Delhi in 2002. In 2005, the Tamil Nadu government was given the 'Excellence Award' for his unrivalled teaching activities and some organization also. He has published more than hundreds of Research Papers and books in the field of Education. At present he is working in the department of Education, Bharathidasan University, Tamil Nadu.

ABOUT THE BOOK

The Bhagavad-Gita says that people under the compulsion of desires, following their own natures, worship other deities with suitable rituals. The supreme God does not frown upon such worship; on the contrary, He deepens their faith in their respective ideals and enables them to obtain the object of their desires. The ultimate fulfillment of desires, however, comes from Him alone who is the real dispenser of the fruits of worship. Education should bring about a change in any individual for the betterment of the society. Individuals in the society are involved in various related activities linked to the individual, family and society. He is forced to voice his opinions and develop his own likes and dislikes. His experience in different situations provides him with a set of moral values and attitudes. The building up of a person's character is closely related to moral anxiety.

❐

Different Facets of Education

Dr. S.K. Panneer Selvam
Assistant Professor, Department of Education
Bharathidasan University, T.N.,India

AMIGA PRESS INC.

AMIGA PRESS INC.
H.O:- 28-A, Indra Park, St.No-9
Near-Chander Nagar, Krishna Nagar
Delhi: - 110051 (India)
Tel: - 011-22504028, +91-98736-57000
Email: - amigapress@gmail.com
info@amigapress.co.in
amigaeditorial@gmail.com
amigapub@gmail.com

Website: - www.amigapress.co.in

This edition is published by Amiga Press Inc.

ISBN: 978-93-84533-61-8

First Published 2020

Printed and bound in India by Replika Press Pvt. Ltd.

Contents

❏❏❏

1

Problem and its Perspectives

"There can be Peace in the world only if the different religions show mutual respect and work for the common good of humanity"

God has made different religions to suit different aspirants, times and countries. All doctrines have many paths; but a path is by no means God Himself. Indeed, one can reach God if one follows any one of the paths; with whole-hearted devotion. Suppose there are errors in the religion that one has accepted; if one is sincere and earnest, then God Himself will correct those errors.

According to Hinduism, no prophet is unique in the sense that he is the greatest of all. All receive their message from the one source and present it to men to suit their particular needs. In the teachings of Christ, Buddha, Mohammed and Krishna one may see apparent differences due to the peculiar requirements of the people whom these prophets taught. But in their communion with reality they all experienced the same goodness, beauty and truth. The common inner experiences of prophets are not noticed by their followers; the apparent external differences in their teachings account for much of religious quarrelling and controversy.

A religion which regards ultimate reality as impersonal truth and at the same time recognizes the validity of its concrete manifestations for the benefit of struggling aspirants cannot but admit the validity of all religious ideals and show them respect. The situation is quite different with those for whom the Personal God is the ultimate reality. To accept the doctrine of exclusive salvation and develop the concept of 'either-or' are natural for them. Hinduism has never developed the theory of a jealous God or exclusive salvation; the idea of a chosen people is alien to it. In the Hindu monotheism all other deities are either absorbed in the Supreme God or accepted as parts of Him. Whereas in the Semitic monotheism they are not tolerated. The Bhagavad-Gita says that people under the compulsion of desires, following their own natures, worship other deities with suitable rituals. The supreme God does not frown upon such worship; on the contrary, He deepens their faith in their respective ideals and enables them to obtain the object of their desires. The ultimate fulfillment of desires, however, comes from Him alone who is the real dispenser of the fruits of worship. To a disciple who criticized the questionable rituals of a certain Hindu sect, Sri Ramakrishna said that the members of that sect, too, if sincere, would enter God's mansion- it might be by the back door. Religion is normally imbibed through education.

Education should bring about a change in any individual for the betterment of the society. Individuals in the society are involved in various related activities linked to the individual, family and society. He is forced to voice his opinions and develop his own likes and dislikes. His experience in different situations provides him with a set of moral values and attitudes. The building up of a person's character is closely related to moral anxiety.

Generally in our society, the moral anxiety can be perceived in the people with various attitudes. Those who are inclined in the path of religion are found to be morally anxious most of the time. The subjective introspection may be continuously occurring in their religious path. Positive or negative responses of religious concepts are prevention of character, faith in God, prayer and worship and are some of the religious attitudes.

EMERGENCE OF THE PROBLEM

Religious beliefs and practices have been a universal feature of human society, ''Men have probably thought about sacred things from the time they began to think at all, but thinking about why one thinks about sacred things is a relatively recent enterprise.

Religion may be defined as man's belief in supernatural forces outside himself, which forces, he is convinced, influence human events. As a concrete experience, religion is accompanied by emotions, especially of fear, awe, or reverence.

The objective or scientific study of the religious life had seemed too many a contradiction in terms, a mere act of violence on the part of scientist toward a sphere of life he does not understand.

Dr. Radhakrishnan (1948) "Religion is not the acceptance of academic abstractions or the celebrations of ceremonies but kind of life and experience. It is an insight into the nature of reality (Dharshana) or experience of reality (Anubhava)." In this book Religion and society' points out that "Religion is necessary to educated man and helps him to rise above his baseness and work upwards" (1952).

He also quoted "Religion is an attitude which gives meaning and unity to existence and it is not a set of dogmas to be universally accepted" in the book called 'Recovery of Faith' (1956).

The attitude towards religion is a positive or negative evaluations, emotional feelings, and action tendencies towards particular religions with respect to social objects. It is a favorable or unfavorable responses involving some kind of actions inherently or overtly towards God.

DIFFERENT RELIGIOUS CONCEPT

Different religions are differing forces in the economy of God; all working for the good of mankind. Different faiths are necessary to suit the diversity of human temperaments. Some men are emotional, some rational, some introspective, some active; again, there are those who wish to contemplate an abstract ideal, and those who wish to worship through concrete symbols. If there were only one religious discipline, there would be no hope for those who did not respond to it. Hence it is fortunate that there are many religions instead of only one, as many would prefer to have it. The greater the number of religions, the more chances people will have to satisfy their spiritual hunger.

The different religions emphasize different facets of the supreme reality. Islam, perhaps more than any other religion, stands for the brotherhood of men among its own devotees. With the Moslems there are no social distinctions. It is inspiring to read about the pilgrimage of the Moslems to Mecca. There hundreds of thousands of the faithful discard their differing dress, whether of prince, ordinary citizen, or beggar, put on the seamless white garment which makes the chieftain indistinguishable from the shepherd, and proceed to the holy shrine to declare their surrender to almighty Allah. Before God all Moslems are equal.

With the Christians the central idea is: 'Watch and pray, for the kingdom of heaven is at hand' – which means, purify your minds and be ready for the coming of the Lord. And one cannot but admire the love of God, which innumerable Christians show through love of men, to whose service they devote their time, energy, and material resources. The idea of 'sharing' is perhaps the most striking feature of Christianity in practice.

Judaism has clung to the idea of God's power and justice and the Jewish people with dauntless patience have faced the ordeals and sufferings through which they have passed for two thousand years without losing their faith in God's power and justice.

Buddhism teaches how to attain peace through renunciation and service. In these days of selfishness and competition, it is a joy to see Buddhist monk serving people with infinite love and infinite compassion, as taught by their prophet.

Hinduism makes the realization of God, who is both within and without, the central fact of life. Thousands of Hindus are willing, even today, to renounce everything- including the world itself- to experience the reality of God.

Human beings differ from one another in size, shape, and colour of skin, but an underlying humanity is common to all. One may not be able to lay one's finger on it, yet it exists all the same. Likewise the universal religion, in the form of God-consciousness, runs through all faiths, whether primitive, ethical, or highly mystical.

Thus the different religions are like different photographs of the same building from different angles; but all of them are genuine pictures. None can exhaust the infinite power, beauty, love, and goodness of God.

MEANING OF RELIGION

Religion is something personal, leading to a larger impersonality of significance which is implanted in the personality of individuals. It is an inward turning of the mind towards its source, gradually by stages, rather than an outward meandering in the social field of work and entertainment, so that the intensity of a religious achievement cannot be observed by outward activity or conduct. .

Religion is nothing but a spirit which you adopt in your life and attitude in general so that, if that is absent, religion becomes a corpse, a skeleton, without flesh and blood in it. It may have all the appearances of a living organism, but it has no life in it. So we can have lifeless religions, yet they may look like religions - just as a dead body may look like a human being, but it is not a human being because it is has lost its value, which is the spirit of existence.

DEFINITION OF RELIGION

There are many definitions of religion, and most have struggled to avoid an overly sharp definition on the one hand, and meaningless generalities on the other. Some have tried to use formalistic, doctrinal definitions and others have tried to use experiential, emotive, intuitive, valuational and ethical factors.

Sociologists and anthropologists see religion as an abstract set of ideas, values, or experiences developed as part of a cultural matrix. Primitive religion was indistinguishable from the sociocultural acts where custom and ritual defined an emotional reality.

Other religious scholars have put forward a definition of religion that avoids the reductionism of the various sociological and psychological disciplines that relegate religion to its component factors. Religion may be defined as the presence of a belief in the sacred or the holy. For example Rudolf Otto's "The Idea of the Holy," formulated in 1917, defines the essence of religious awareness as awe, a unique blend of fear and fascination before the divine. Friedrich Schleiermacher in the late 18th century defined religion as a "feeling of absolute dependence."

The Concise Oxford Dictionary (1990) defines religion as "Human recognition of superhuman controlling power and especially of a personal God entitled to obedience." This definition would not consider some Buddhist sects as religions. Many Unitarian Universalists are excluded by this description. Strictly interpreted, it would also reject polytheistic religions, since it refers to "a personal God."

Merriam-Webster's Online Dictionary defines the religion as "A cause, principle, or system of beliefs held to with ardor and faith." This is a curious definition because it does not require elements often associated with religion, such as deity, morality, worldview, etc. Also it requires that a person pursue their religion with enthusiasm. Many people identify themselves with a specific religion, but are not intensely engaged with their faith.

Webster's New World Dictionary (Third College Edition): "Any specific system of belief and worship, often involving a code of ethics and a philosophy." This definition would exclude religions that do not engage in worship. It implies that there are two important components to religion:

This dual nature of religion is expressed clearly in the Christian Scriptures (New Testament) in Matthew 22:36-39: "Teacher, what is the great commandment in the law? Jesus said unto him, Thou shalt love the Lord thy God with all thy heart, and with all thy soul, and with thy entire mind. This is the first and great commandment. And the second is like unto it, Thou shalt love thy neighbor as thyself."

DEFINITION OF RELIGION BY ACADEMICIANS

Alfred North Whitehead defines religion as: "what the individual does with his own solitariness." Religion can be further defined as: "... a system of social coherence based on a common group of beliefs or attitudes concerning an object, person, unseen being, or system of thought considered to be supernatural, sacred, divine or highest truth, and the moral codes, practices, values, institutions, traditions, and rituals associated with such belief or system of thought."

Clifford G. defined religion as a cultural system meaning, "A religion is a system of symbols which acts to establish powerful, pervasive, and long-lasting moods and motivations in men by formulating conceptions of a general order of existence and clothing these conceptions with such an aura of factuality that the moods and motivations seem uniquely realistic."

Don Swenson defines religion in terms of the sacred as, "Religion is the individual and social experience of the sacred that is manifested in mythologies, ritual, ethos, and integrated into a collective or organization."

Paul Connelly also defines religion in terms of the sacred and the spiritual aspect meaning, "Religion originates in an attempt to represent and order beliefs, feelings, imaginings and actions that arise in response to direct experience of the sacred and the spiritual. As this attempt expands in its formulation and elaboration, it becomes a process that creates meaning for itself on a sustaining basis, in terms of both its originating experiences and its own continuing responses."

THE CONCEPT OF RELIGIOUS ATTITUDE

Religious attitude is a positive or a negative response or tendency towards various aspects or religion like faith in God, the knowledge that the soul is different from the body, preservation of character, formal religion, priest, future life, spirits and spirit world.

An important attitude is response or reaction to the value. It is a favorable or an unfavorable response involving some kind of action inherently or overtly towards God. The existence of an attitude towards something is quite impossible without having the knowledge about the thing.

VARIOUS ASPECTS OF RELIGION

i. Nature of God

Every religion has its own adoption of God. The ways and means, the rites and sacrifices may vary, but the supremacy of God was always unquestionable and indisputable. God is the creator ruler, and supreme authority of all the times. The most essential aspect of God is his cosmic nature. God has been conceived by people of various religions as both as personal and impersonal and also immanent and transcendent. He reveals himself through incarnations to the world. He is the creator and destroyer. He is the Supreme Being. He is full of perfection. He is the cause of all cosmic change yet he remains unchanged. God is omnipresent, Omniscient and Omni potential. He is the redeemer of souls.

ii. Prayer and worship

Prayer and worship are important religious activities practiced in every religion. The human soul cries to a power that can help him when he is in need. Prayer is a humble request to God. It is a religious observance, public or private. Veneration to supernatural is displayed through appropriate acts, rites or ceremonies. A form of adoration to pay respect is divine worship.

iii. Priests

In almost all religions, religious activities are performed by priests of some type. The priests exercise great influence upon the people. They dominate all religious function, both inside and outside the temples, churches and mosques on all sacred occasions.

iv. Future Life

The ultimate aim in leading a spiritual life is attainment of Moksha, Nirvana or a life after death. All religions speak about the present life with future orientation. Hindus speak about the transformation of human consciousness into divine consciousness which is possible only by breaking the cycle of birth and rebirth. For Christians life in this world ends with death but it is the beginning of life with Christ. Church is a group of pilgrims marching towards the heavenly Jerusalem.

v. Formal Religion

All religions have got a formal aspect related to it. It is mainly concerned with the structure of the religion. The scripture, place of worship, festivals, patterns of rites etc. constitute the structure of whatever religion one practices.

vi. Spirits and Spirit World

The general meaning of spirit is that which gives life to the physical organism in contrast to its purely material element, the breadth of life. Hinduism has faith in the existence of spirits which can visit the world and can have contact with people. The notion of spirit is world wide and discussed in every religion. Spirits are invisible and can bring good or evil to man.

RELIGIOUS BELIEF

Religious belief usually relates to the existence, nature and worship of a deity or deities and divine involvement in the universe and human life. Alternately, it may also relate to values and practices transmitted by a spiritual leader. Unlike other belief systems, which may be passed on orally, religious belief tends to be codified in literate societies; religion in non-literate societies is still largely passed on orally. Religious beliefs are found in virtually every society throughout human history.

SPIRITUALITY

Members of an organized religion may not see any significant difference between religion and spirituality. Or they may see a distinction between the mundane, earthly aspects of their religion and its spiritual dimension.Some individuals draw a strong distinction between religion and spirituality. They may see spirituality as a belief in ideas of religious significance such as God, the Soul, or Heaven, but not feel bound to the bureaucratic structure and creeds of a particular organized religion. They choose the term spirituality rather than religion to describe their form of belief, perhaps reflecting disillusionment with organized religion and a movement towards a more modern more tolerant and more intuitive form of religion.

MYTH

The word myth has several meanings.A traditional stories of ostensibly historical events that serves to unfold part of the world view of a people or explain a practice, belief, or natural phenomenon; can be termed as a myth. A person or thing having only an imaginary or unverifiable existence is usually referred to as a myth. A metaphor for the spiritual potentiality in the human being is said to be a myth in the minds of educators.

RELIGIONS AS ABSOLUTELY TRUE

Religions can be viewed as absolutely and unchangingly true. Jewish and Christian and religions model which hold that God relates to humanity through covenants that he established a covenant with all humanity at the time of Noah called the Noahide Laws, and that he established a covenant with Israel through the Ten Commandments, and also Jesus Christ did establish a covenant with his people through the New Testament. Exclusivists hold that one particular set of religious doctrines is the "One True Religion," and all others are false to the extent that they conflict with the true one, so that the development of the True Religion is tied inexorably to one prophet or holy book. All other religions are seen as either distortions of the original truth or original fabrications resulting from either human ignorance or imagination, or a more devious influence, such as false prophets or the influence of another rival supernatural entity such as Satan. Man kinds to be over ruled by this absolute both in religion.

Religions faith and positive attitude to words religion usually help people to develop a less anxious and more tolerant personality features. The deep faith one develops over the process of experience in this own religious beliefs can lay the foundation for a better conscious effort to over curve situations that could cause over anxiousness.

DEFINITIONS OF ANXIETY

Anxiety according to Mower, "is a learned response, occurring to signals which are unconditioned stimuli that are premonitory to situations of injury or pain."Anxiety is an emotional and non-adjective response which a person is making to his conflicts. In dealing with anxiety status Mac Curdy (1925) writes, "The anxiety is directed against mental images of a dangerous nature which in psychosis comes in to full consciousness. The fear, as such, is rational, if the reality of the stimulus were only granted".

According to Freud, "anxiety is a consequence of the frustration of needs, particularly the frustration that occurs in conflict situations". Freudian theory also says that a person is largely unaware of the sources or causes of anxiety, but that psychoanalysis helps the patient uncover the sources of conflict in his or her previous history.

In motivational terms anxiety is anticipation of pain, psychological or physical. This definition has three components: First of all the definition classifies the nature of the state, namely, a state of apprehension or distress; then the nature of the stimulus is given, namely, a real or imagined threat, and finally the definition tells what is threatened, namely, the self.

Anxiety can be defined as an individual's fear laden overreaction, to an adjustment situation. The threatening implications of the situations are felt because the individual already sense that he cannot cope with the situation. It becomes a threat to his self esteem. 1925, defines anxiety as, "Mental distress with respect to some anticipated frustrations".

THE CONCEPT OF MORAL ANXIETY

Anxiety is an unpleasant, emotional state of high energy that involves a complex combination of emotions that include fear, apprehension, and worry. It is often accompanied by physical sensations such as heart palpitations, nausea, chest pain, shortness of breath, or tension headache.

Anxiety is often described as having cognitive, somatic, emotional, and behavioral components (Seligman, Walker & Rosenhan, 2001). The cognitive component entails expectation of a diffuse and uncertain danger. Somatically the body prepares the organism to deal with threat (known as an emergency reaction): blood pressure and heart rate are increased, sweating is increased, bloodflow to the major muscle groups is increased, and immune and digestive system functions are inhibited. Externally, somatic signs of anxiety may include pale skin, sweating, trembling, and pupillary dilation.

Emotionally, anxiety causes a sense of dread or panic and physically causes nausea, and chills. Behaviorally, both voluntary and involuntary behaviors may arise directed at escaping or avoiding the source of anxiety.

These behaviors are frequent and often maladaptive, being most extreme in anxiety disorders. However, anxiety is not always pathological or maladaptive: it is a common emotion along with fear, anger, sadness, and happiness, and it has a very important function in relation to survival. Anxiety can be somewhat of a mental illness.

DEVELOPMENT OF MORALITY

While some philosophers, psychologists and evolutionary biologists hold that morality is a thin crust hiding egoism, amorality, and anti-social tendencies, others see morality as equally a product of evolutionary forces and as evidence for continuity with other group-living organisms. One approach argues that moral codes are founded on emotional instincts and intuitions that were naturally selected in the past because they aided survival and reproduction (inclusive fitness), and that they still generally prescribe behavior that enhances individual fitness and/or group well-being. Selected psychological and behavioral tendencies, and their abstraction in to moral codes or religions, are seen to be common to most or all human cultures.

MORAL CODES

Moral codes are often complex definitions of right and wrong that are based upon well-defined value systems. They dictate proper personal conduct. Although some people might think that a moral code is simple, rarely is there anything simple about one's values, ethics, etc. or, for that matter, the judgment of those of others. The difficulty lies in the fact that morals are often part of a religion and more often than not about culture codes. Sometimes, moral codes give way to legal codes, which couple penalties or corrective actions with particular practices. Note that while many legal codes are merely built on a foundation of religious and/or cultural moral codes, ofttimes they are one and the same.

Examples of moral codes include the Golden Rule; the Noble Eightfold Path of Buddhism; the ancient Egyptian code of Ma'at ;the ten commandments of Judaism, Christianity, and Islam; the yamas and niyama of the Hindu scriptures; the ten Indian commandments; and the principle of the Dessek.

Another related concept is the moral core which is assumed to be innate in each individual, to those who accept that differences between individuals are more important than Creators or their rules. This, in some religious systems (e.g. Taoism and Gnosticism), is assumed to be the basis of all aesthetics and thus moral choice. Moral codes as such are therefore seen as coercive part of human politics.

MORALITY IN JUDICIAL SYSTEMS

The law is considered a living governing system constructed by present and historical debate and moral consensus among juries, and more generally, all citizens under the system. This system is used to maintain order, righteousness, and justice in everyday life. Individual actions or events can be summoned to court for review, investigation, and prosecution if it is believed that there has been a breach of morality (meaning, a violation of the law) or if a law's moral implication is questioned. A verdict is a lawful determination of guilt, and a guilty party is one that has committed an immoral act.

In most systems, the lack of morality of the individual can also be a sufficient cause for punishment, or can be an element for the grading of the punishment. Especially in the systems where modesty (i.e., with reference to sexual crimes) is legally protected or otherwise regulated, the definition of morality as a legal element and in order to determine the cases of infringement, is usually left to the vision and appreciation of the single judge and hardly ever precisely specified. In such cases, it is common to verify an application of the prevalent common morality of the interested community that consequently becomes enforced by the law for further reference.

The government of South Africa is attempting to create a Moral Regeneration movement. Part of this is a proposed Bill of Morals, which will bring a biblical-based "moral code" into the realm of law. This move by a nominally secular democracy has attracted relatively little criticism.

ANXIETY AND EGO-DEFENSE MECHANISMS

In Freud's view, the human is driven towards tension reduction, in order to reduce feelings of anxiety. Anxiety an aversive inner state that people seek to avoid or escape. Humans seek to reduce anxiety through defense mechanisms. Defense Mechanisms can be psychologically healthy or maladaptive, but tension reduction is the overall goal in both cases. A comprehensive list of Defense Mechanisms was developed by Anna Freud, Sigmund's daughter.

Anna remained with her Father throughout his life, never marrying. In Freudian terms, she remained trapped in her Oedipus complex, never giving up her longing to possess her father sexually. However, because of a strong ego and super ego, this id based desires were sublimated into psychological creativity which advanced Freudian theory, her father's greatest love.

FREUD SPECIFIED THREE MAJOR TYPES OF ANXIETY

Reality Anxiety: the most basic form, rooted in reality. Fear of a dog bite, fear arising from an impending accident. (Ego Based Anxiety) Most Common Tension Reduction Method: Removing oneself from the harmful situation.

Neurotic Anxiety: Anxiety which arises from an unconscious fear that the libidinal impulses of the id will take control at an in opportune time. This type of anxiety is driven by a fear of punishment that will result from expressing the id's desires without proper sublimation.

Moral Anxiety: Anxiety which results from fear of violating moral or societal codes, moral anxiety appears as guilt or shames this conception of Anxiety; can be seen as a reason why Freud concentrated on strengthening the Ego through psychoanalysis.

Defense Mechanisms

When some type of anxiety occurs, the mind responds in two ways:

First, problem solving efforts are increased, and secondly, defense mechanisms are triggered. These are tactics which the Ego develops to help deal with the id and the Super Ego. All Defense Mechanisms share two common properties:

1. They can operate unconsciously
2. They can distort, transform, or falsify reality is some way.
3. The changing of perceived reality allows for a lessening of anxiety, reducing the psychological tension felt by an individual.

NEED FOR THE STUDY

According to Gandhiji, for the all-round development of the child, education should provide the right understanding about attitude and morality among the students. Particularly during the adolescent age, the maturity level usually develops and awareness about morality and religious values also begins to emerge. It is also evident that during this stage, lot of anxiety and stress is revealed. This could be due to the lack of understanding about morality. For the purpose of getting more insight into this concept, there is a need to study the moral anxiety and religious attitude of students at the secondary school level.

If clarity of the various aspects related to the moral anxiety and religious attitude is unearthed, students at the secondary level can be helped to develop the right level of moral anxiety and also a positive religious attitude.

STATEMENT OF THE PROBLEM

Religious Attitude and Moral Anxiety among the Higher Secondary School Students".

OPERATIONAL DEFINITIONS

Religious Attitude

The investigator defines religious attitude as attitude towards religion and its concepts in students. Religious attitude in this study refers to the scores obtained by using the Religious Attitude scale designed by Rajamanickam (1966).

Moral Anxiety

This study refers to the 'anxiety towards morality' in students. By this, the investigator means the scores obtained by administering the scale of Moral Anxiety standardized by Lawrence R.Good and Katherine C.Good.

Higher Secondary School Students

Higher Secondary school students in this study refer to the students studying in XI and XII classes.

OBJECTIVES OF THE STUDY

- To find out the level of Religious attitude of higher secondary school students.
- To find out the level of moral anxiety of higher secondary school students.
- To find out the significant difference between boys and girls of higher secondary school in their religious attitude.
- To find out the significant difference between students studying in standard XIth and XIIth in their religious attitude.
- To find out the significant difference between students studying in English and Tamil medium of the higher secondary schools in their religious attitude.
- To find out the significant difference between students studying in Government and Private higher secondary schools in their religious attitude.
- To find out the significant difference between boys and girls of higher secondary schools in their moral anxiety.
- To find out the significant difference between students studying in standard XIth and XIIth in their moral anxiety.
- To find out the significant difference between student studying in English and Tamil medium of the higher secondary schools in their moral anxiety.
- To find out the significant difference between students studying in Government and Private higher secondary school in their moral anxiety.

- To find out the relationship between religious attitude and moral anxiety of higher secondary school students.

LIMITATIONS OF THE STUDY

Due to lack of time and resources available the study has been limited to the following.

1. The present investigation is confined to the students studying in Higher Secondary school level 7XIth & XIIth.
2. The study has been restricted only to the students studying in government schools and private schools.
3. The study has been limited to Dharmapuri District, (Tamil Nadu) only.
4. The study has been limited to English and Tamil Medium only.
5. It includes a sample size of 300 higher secondary school students only.

CONCLUSION

The first chapter is chiefly concerned with the conceptual frame work of the problem chosen for the study. This chapter gives an overview of the problem, its statement, and its significance. It also includes the objectives, and limitations of the study. It also gives an elaborate explanation of the meaning of the terms, religious attitude and moral anxiety.

❐

2

Review of Related Literature

In this chapter, the related literature enfolds studies related to the variables used in the present investigation. After going through the related studies regarding the religious attitude and moral anxiety among the HigherSecondarySchool students the researcher can conceptualize the research problem clearly and precisely.

According to Best (1963), the familiarity with the literature in any problem area helps the students to discover, the known facts, the attempted methods and the manner in which the problems are solved. The investigator feels that the study of related literature helps in acquiring information about the studies done in the field, avoid duplication and further guides in carrying out the investigation successfully. In the following chapter, a review is made on the studies conducted in India and abroad related to the present study.

STUDIES RELATD TO RELIGIOUS ATTITUDE

Studies Done Abroad

Horne and William Stender.H (1945) administered a questionnaire containing observation of daily prayer, Holy Communion, church going and practice of baptism to denominational and non-denominational college students. It was found out that denominational students tend towards religious orthodoxy those non-denominational students.

The study by Telford (1950) on ten thousands students at the University of Utah tried to correlate religious background of the student the degree of antagonism toward church. It was found out that females were more favourable to church and that church attitude was found positively related to church affiliation and attendance.

Weima, J. (1965) of Catholic University of Nijmegen. Netherlands examined authoritarianism, religious conservatism and socio centric attitudes in Roman Catholic groups. A Dutch version of F. scale and Anti-Semitic Scale, an anti-protestant scale and a religious conservatism scale were used to evaluate attitudes in catholic students. Measures of authoritarianism were found to correlate positively with measures of Anti-Semitism, anti-communism and religious conservatism. Difference is examined in the light of official catholic attitudes to jews and protestants. It is positive in both cases. A study by Robert Young, K., David Dustin, S. Holtzman and Wayne H. (1996) of the University of Texas investigated change in attitude towards religion in a Southern University. This describes study changes in attitude towards organised religion as measured in three surveys taken over a periods of nine year. The attitude of the respondents who in each survey were under graduate students at the University / of Texas became less favourable towards organised religion during that period. Several variables were found to be related to attitude towards organised religion. These include sex, grade point average major academic field, religious preference, and frequency of church attendance.

John Kottman, E. (1966) University of Lowa conducted a semantic study of religious attitude. During 1965, one hundred and forty one male and twenty six female students at the University of Lowa participated in testing the hypothesis that a positive correlation exists between intension and religious attitude. In general sematic terminology "one who relies largely on words and disregards observations is said to have an intentional orientation". Five kinds of intentional manifestations were measured by one scale; also administered were excerpts from three test designed to measure attitudes towards God, the Bible, and Church. In order to avoid bias religious affiliations were not asked for. These data supports hypothesis that persons who are most intentional tend to have the strongest religious attitude. Although the correlations; not high, they point to the existence of the hypothesized connection.

Pang, Henry (1968) of Middle Bury College examined religious attitudinal dimensions of altruism, conformity, devotion, fundamentalism, mysticism, superstition, and total religiosity in 10 students denominational groups of eighty students.. It was generalized that the Ss would reflect attitudes of their respective denominations. The groups differed in mysticism ($P<0.05$) and the other dimensions ($P>0.01$).

Maranell, Gary, M. (1968) of the University Kansas made a factor analytic study of some selected dimensions of religious attitude. Eight conceptually distinct / dimension of religious attitude were translated into attitude scales. The religious attitude of urban clergy men of eleven denominations in four regions of the country was surveyed. Resulting scale scores were correlated for the total population and the resulting correlation matrix was factor analysed. The factors were orthogonally rotated. The two factors were (1) a conservative fundamentalist attitude cluster and (2) a more liberal socially concerned religious attitude factor.

John Roscoe (1968) investigated religious beliefs of American College Students. This study is part of a research study of student values. One thousand five students from seventeen colleges and universities returned the polyphasic values inventory (PVI). The schools included major universities, teachers colleges and liberal art colleges. Two of the twenty multiple-choice questions of PVI sampled student's religious beliefs. 52 percent of the students were protestant, 25 percent Catholic, 12 percent with no religious affiliation and 5 percent were Jewish. 73 percent of the students expressed belief in personnel God. Of the 73 percent 28 percent subscribed to the traditional Judeo-Christian concept of the God of Bible. 88 percent of the catholic and 83 percent of the Protestants expressed belief in a personnel God. Jewish students were more liberal in their beliefs than Christian Students. 24 percent of students considered the Bible as the inspired religious book, not all of which is completely realizable but which directs men's thought towards God.

Thomas Thai, V. (1969) made an investigation of religious attitudes, ideals, and personality traits of the four groups of catholic college students. The religious attitude scale, the test in ideals, the Guilford-Zimmerman Temperament survey and information questionnaires were used to test the students with regard to their religious attitudes, ideals, personality traits and backgrounds. The subjects were eight hundred and eighty four catholic men and women, fresh men and women, fresh men and seminars, students enrolled at twenty two catholic and non catholic college and universities of New York. Men students were, however found to score significantly higher in the ideal of altruistic interest, on self interest and on social approval. Significant difference between the mean religion attitudes, religious values, altruistic interest, emotional stability and personal relations were found in favour of women students. Women students excelled the n on students in their religious practices of the students participated in the study about 83 percent of the men and 90 percent of the women, stated that religion had influenced their individual lives either "very strongly" or "strongly". Pearson product moment co-efficient of correlation were found to be significant at the 0.01 level between religious attitude and religious values, between religious values and some personality traits namely, restraint, emotional stability, friendliness, and personal relations.

In a study by Prezyna, Wlady Slaw (1969), investigated the relationship between the religious attitude and personality characteristics. The religious attitude scale applied in the study was constructed by the author. Personality was investigated with sixteen PF in its polish version standardized on polish – population. The sample consisted on sixty women and forty men. Results reveal the high positive religious intensity group to possess on the average more emotional maturity, more super ego control greater, self control, higher sensitivity and contact with the environment. The lower group was characterized by the opposite features.

Hcpburn and Lawrence R. (1971), found that systematic information concerning adolescent views towards religions is very limited though at least one study reported as early as one thousand and nine hundred perceptively related the general nature of adolescence to an undefined sense of incompleteness. Religious interest ranks high among adolescent students but it is not nearly so marked among non student peers. Conflict between liberal religious teachings and scientific views of the world appears to be implicated in adolescent students concern over religion. Since commitment has many dimensions, it poses measurement difficulties. Some investigators define dimensions of religion as belief, practice, experience knowledge, and consequence or effect in every day life. Development of valid approaches to the academic study and religion can provide expanded educational opportunities since religion elicit attitudinal responses from people whether or not they are religious.

Lewis, et.al., investigated religiosity among Indo-Chinese students for about 400 in Utah. Findings showed that the major students adopted western Christian Religions in which most of them affiliated with ethnic congregation. Religion rate was important in their life and reported high amount of religious participation.

Ponton, et.al, (1988) administrated the religious oriented inventor, the quest scales (Baston C.D. 1976) and a culturally adapted social distance scale to a Venezuelan sample of two hundred and seventy five University Students. The results indicated the extrinsic religiosity correlated positively. With prejudice, intrinsic religiosity correlated negatively.

Boisvert, Donald Luc undertook a sociological study of religion and nationalism in Quebec society. He argues that religion was a stage for the expression and unification of three sets of polarities found within Quebec society. Nationalism versus religion, the elite versus the masses and popular religiosity versus clerical authority. The review of the relationship between the Catholic Church and Quebac society was dealt with and the basic foundation for the subsequent analysis were made by religion.

Deonandan, Kalovvatie (1990) conducted a study on Religion and the struggle for Hegemony in Nicaragua in the University of Queen in Kingston. The thesis established the Church's counter-revolutionary offensive had undermined the position of the liberation theology advocates a id weakened the church bused communities. The revolutionary religions to promote progressive changes in Nicaraguan

Loewenthal, et. al., (1993) made their study on Family size; religiosity and contextually assessed stress were examined in relation to eleven symptoms of depression in fifty six orthodox Jewish women. The major findings were the religiosity and family size were highly confounded, but the effects did differ. Religiosity related to the absence of several symptoms, there is association between family size, religiosity and depressive symptoms.

Krause, Neal (1993) made his study regarding measuring religiosity, which consists of organizational religiosity, subjective religiosity and religious beliefs. His sample size was 936 individuals. The findings examined the impact of religiosity on feelings of life satisfaction among adults.

Francis, Leaslie J. (1993) made his studies on personality and Religion among college students in United Kingdom. The samples of one hundred and twenty six undergraduates were tested using the scale of attitude to Christianity. According to him, the findings had an inverse relationship between psychotism and religiosity, while neither neurotism nor extraversion is positively or negatively related to religiosity.

Gaston and Brown L.B. (1993) studied on heterogeneous groups of Australian one hundred and five female ninety five male including high school and University students Catholic and Anglican church goers and senior citizens using free response and rating of gender based traits show that religion and non-religious prototype are gender typed since Ss assigned to feminine traits to religious target person and masculine traits to non religious target persons. The prototype may make it easier for women to be religious that it to men.

Charies (1993) investigated the dimensionality of religion in the prediction of self reported religious behaviour through the differentiation of religiousness into measure of belief and motivation. One hundred and sixty one students at Christian Protestant colleges participated. Religious belief was measured through eleven primary god concept factors. Both motivation and god concept factors significantly added predictive variance over each other with respect to self reported religious belief.

Medoff, and et.al., (1993) investigated the relationship between deviant social behaviour and membership in fundamentalist Christian denominations at the state level. Four dependent variables arc used to measure deviant social behaviour (1) Murder rate (2) Suicide rate (3) Divorce rate (4) Abortion rate.

The rate of deviant social behaviour is hypothesized to be a function of the states socio economic characteristics and an index of religious fundamentalist attitudes. The results show that fundamentalism has a significant effect on sexual morality, abortion, birth rates and marriage.

Brinkley Ellen. H. (1995), made a study on, "Faith in the world: examining religious right attitudes about texts". It described theological views about written texts, related attitudes exhibited by current protestors, and attitudes created for English language arts teachers. The study suggested that an awareness of the religious perspective might help to lead to more constructive outcomes to the conflicts among teachers, individual students and parents.

Indian Studies

Adinarayan S.P. and Rajamanickam M. (1962) conducted a study on Attitude towards religion, and spiritual and the supernatural belief of the students. The sample of 300 students from Annamalai University was tested by attitude towards religious scale by the investigator. The major findings were: students belonging to higher socio economic level expressed religious attitude more than the students of lower. Rural and urban backgrounds influenced the religious socio-economic level. Rural and urban backgrounds influenced the religious attitude of the students.

A study by Dutt, N.K. (1965) Punjab University, Chandigarh, investigated attitudes of the University students towards religion. A 30 item Likert scale was prepared for eighty two items after item analysis. Results of the final scale on two hundred students showed that girls were significantly more religious than boys. No difference was found due to academic discipline.

Rajamanickam, M.(1966) made his study of religious and related attitudes of the students and professional groups in south India for his Ph.D. in Annamalai University. The sample of 1400 students from Andhra, Kerala, Madras, and Mysore were collected by using the tool Religious Attitude scale constructed by the investigator. The major findings were religious attitude was correlated with conservatism in both the groups, and it was highest for the arts students. Students were more religious than professionals. Men students went to places of worship more than the women students.

Tandom, B.K. (1967) conducted his study on the attitude towards religion of higher secondary school students in Uttar Pradesh towns. A sample of 3917 students, both boys and girls from twenty one towns of Uttar Pradesh were selected for the study. The tools used were the Attitude scale of fifty items by the investigator and Saxena's supplementary questionnaire to the Attitude scale of Religion and Adjustment inventory. The major findings were: Students in general had a favorable attitude towards religion. The communities having favorable religious attitude in the descending order were Hindu, Muslim, Sikh and Christian.

Kapil, H.K. and Aggarwal, Sushma (1967) studied changing pattern of values amongst women in modern Hindu society. A study of ninety six women revealed a definite trend of decline in traditional values to the peripheral area. More than ninety three percent of the respondents expressed absolute faith in transmigration of souls and religious scriptures and ninety five percent supported religious observances. Conversely, except for a lukewarm traditional support for disapproval of divorce, there was a definite decline in the time honoured value of joint family system or disapproval of nuclear family non acceptance of women as the bread earner or giving her equal right of education with man.

The study by Misra, S.L. (1970) made a comparative study of religion-caste differences in concept formation ability of Young adults. Hypothesized that Hindu and Muslim students would different their concept formation ability and difference would be found between Hindu Caste and Muslim sects. Two hundred and eighty eight, 14-19 years old students were selected. Twenty four students represented each of the Hindu caste and student's seventy students represented each of the two Muslim sects. Lovell's concept formation test and Trist Hargreave's tests were administered. On both tests Muslim students scored Higher than Hindu students No significant difference is found with in the groups, although the Hindu castes differed from the scheduled castes on both the tests wish the scheduled castes scoring lower.

This study by Telode, R.D. and R.V. Dable (1980) was conducted on religiosity as a function of sex and type of education. This study was conducted / on under graduate students of which 30 were science students and thirty were arts students. Sample was also selected to include fifteen boys and fifteen girls among arts and science students. Bushans (1971) religiosity scale was used. The study revealed that

1. Arts students were more religious than science students.
2. Girls are more religious than boys.

Gupta A., (1980) conducted a study on relationship between religious attitude and mental health of the Tibetian adolescents. His major objectives of the study were to establish. The tools employed were the Religiosity questionnaire locally constructed by the investigator. The major findings were found to be religious, mentally healthy and possessing positive personality character ties in being warm hearted, self sufficient, controlled and tense.

Hassan M.K. and Khalique (1981) conducted a study on religiosity and its correlates among college students. The samples of four hundred and eighty college students from Ranchi Univeristy were tested by using scale of

Religiosity. Some of the major findings were: Muslims tend to have higher degree of religiosity than Hindus. The sex did not influence religious attitude of both Hindus and Muslims. Positive correlation between religiosity and anxiety was reported.

Rizvi, S.A.H (1986) conducted thesis for his Ph.D. in Alligarh Muslim University. His study was on attitudes towards religious education in relation to certain value orientations. The sample was 200 postgraduate students of the Hindu and Muslim communities in the Alligarh Muslim University. They were tested by using the tools Rajamanickam's religious attitude scale. It was found that the majority of students had moderate attitude towards religious education. Irrespective of the difference in their gender, socio-economic status and religion students had similar view.

Roquiya Zainuddin (1994) attempted to know the level of religiosity and spiritually in relation to certain personality needs. The major aspect of this study is concerned with the relationship between the spiritual orientation and personality needs based on Murrya's classification of psychogenic need on one hand, and religiosity and needs on the other hand. The sample consisted of two hundred and twenty teachers of various faculties. The tools used were (1) Meenakshi Personality Inventory (2). Religiosity scale and (3) Spiritual Orientation Inventory. Multiple regression analysis was sued to treat the data. The results revealed that aggression was found to be a significant factor of spirituality. The N-achievement was a significant negative predictor of religiosity and the need-exhibition was a significant positive contributor to religiosity.

Sayed Flroj and S. Karunanidhi (1995) Madras University attempted to find out the of foot of religious (y on values. The sample was selected from the students of various colleges Madras University. The data were collected by using Rajamanicak's Religious Attitude Scale (1989) and the value scale developed by Malla Reddy (1992). Results of the study show that those who are high on religiosity were found to traditional in their values. Whereas low A religiosity people are modern in their in their values.

STUDIES RELATED TO MORAL ANXIETY

Studies Done Abroad

Sigmund Freud (1995) describes how the ego is a range of mechanisms to handle the conflict between the Id, the ego and the super ego, which is why they are often called 'Ego-Defense Mechanisms'. He has discussed elaborately on anxiety and tension.

1. Moral anxiety
2. Neurotic anxiety

3. Objective anxiety

Kierkegaard (1959) relates anxiety decision, commitment, choice, and awareness. Wherever there is a decision or an opportunity to actualize a possibility, there is anxiety. In order for self-development to advance, anxiety must be experienced. Anxiety is referred to as a "school" and as "one of the best teachers", since through facing anxiety, awareness is increased. The normal person faces anxiety and moves ahead. The neurotic is viewed as a "shut-up" person, who constricts his awareness and individuality in order to avoid anxiety, and thereby becomes automation.

Feldhusen, Denny and Condon (1965) investigated the difference between high and low anxious children in convergent and divergent thinking and found that the difference on divergent thinking was non significant among the children.

Justice Maclene Carol (1989) made a study on "The Effect of Literature instruction with an emphasis on Kohlberg's moral development stages on secondary students' moral reasoning, and abilities'. Major purpose of the investigation was to determine whether there were significant differences in moral reasoning between groups of students who received literature instruction emphasizing on Lawrence Kohlberg's moral stages of development (experimental) and a group of students who received instruction by conventional teaching (control). An additional purpose of the investigation was to determine whether this teaching strategy depends on students' intelligence, writing skills etc. In the findings of the investigation, literature course which contained moral reasoning of students was below the mean intelligence scores on the test of moral development.

Wilhelm et al (1989) studied about fear and anxiety in low vision and totally blind children and education for the visually handicapped. They selected one hundred and thirty nine visually impaired children of age group 6-16 years. They were administered on a fear survey and a Manifest Anxiety scale. Students were classified into totally blind and low vision groups. Fear and anxiety scores were similar to those classifications. The general level of anxiety for the total sample when compared with general population showed that fear of students tends to reflect concern for injury to the body.

Jainvely (1991) examined the subjective construction of morality in the prevailing social atmosphere and argued that attribution of responsibility was involved in moral judgment. Responsibility was understood in direct ways and the social perspective also influenced further attribution. Data, supporting the social aspects of moral judgment were also presented in this study, in which sixty four Indian college teachers responded to a modified version of Lawrence Kohlberg's Heniz Dilemma. Traditional Indian (Hindu) thought or morality was also discussed along with the implications for the moral development.

Cart, Wright, Robert, H. and Stephen (1992) investigated on 'social control in alternative religions-A familiar perspective'. In the study the family models were pervasive in both the theological self conceptions of alternative religious organizations and the sociological scholarship on them. It around that the models provided useful directions for studying alternative religions. Since both the institutions frequently enmesh their members in contrasting social environments, it facilitated the occurrence of sustained systematic abuse.

Wilson, Kenneth and Deborah, K. (1992) studied on the 'Moral judgment development for the effect of education and occupation', presenting various conceptualization of moral judgment development which was synthesized into a single longitudinal study. As hypothesized, adolescent moral judgment development and educational attainment exerted significant direct effects on adult moral judgment development. Moral judgment development occupational attainment exerted significant direct effect indirectly through career satisfaction and work related variables. There were also equal to or greater than educational attainments in the pre- directive power.

Taylor et al (1992) made a study on 'Theoretical and therapeutic considerations for the anxiety disorders', which reviewed the theoretical and therapeutic considerations for four types of anxiety disorders: Panic disorder, generalized anxiety, social phobia and obsessive-compulsive disorder. Emphasis was placed on the physiological commitments and neuropsychological bases of these illnesses. Furthermore, pharmacological treatment was related to the underlying substrate of the disorder, which was never possible.

Indian Studies

Pandit K.W. (1964) studied the role of anxiety in academic learning and achievement of school boys. The sample consisted of 145 boys from an elementary school in Delhi. The important findings were: 1. anxiety had a negative relationship with learning and academic achievement; subjects having less anxiety were found to be superior in learning and achievement irrespective of the task difficulty to those having more anxiety. 2. High learners and achievement in the retest, while the highest anxiety group showed poor performance in the retest. 4. Subjects with low intelligence and high anxiety did not improve in achievement upto the expectation as a result of induced anxiety. 5. Better achievement did not act as reinforcement in improving achievement of high anxious low achievers. Anxiety interfered with the retention of learning.

Patel A.D. (1977) collected total sample of876 student teachers, both male and female, from thirteen colleges of education. Stratified random sampling technique was followed. It was found that the relationship of anxiety and achievement between student teachers was negative but not significant. The mean performance of the high and the low anxiety group was 47.6percent and 50.2percent respectively.

Annamma A.K.(1980) studied on the value, aspirations and adjustment of college students in Kerala. The major findings were: 1. A majority of the college students were conformists with a stable system of values and without rebellious tendencies. 2. The younger college students were more oriented to spiritualism as compared to the older group, which were more materialism oriented. 3. The academic achievement, residential background and father's education and occupational status had no relationship to value orientation of college students.

Ramachandran (1989) investigation the influence of anxiety and adjustment on performance. The main objective of the study was to find out the relationship between academic performance and anxiety. The major finding of the study was that there was low negative correlation between academic performance and anxiety.

Gupta, Rajan 1989) (investigated on the values and moral judgement of adolescents of two representative centers of western and eastern states of Uttar Pradesh. The sample of the study covered eighty boys and eighty girls. The tool used was Moral Judgement Test developed by the researcher. The major findings were: Regional differences influenced the different personal values of adolescents; regional differences influenced different personal values of adolescents; regional differences influenced different moral judgement areas of adolescents.

Namrata (1992) conducted a study on two hundred and one boys and two hundred and eight girls, to find out the relationship between personality traits, stress, anxiety and achievement. The major findings was that the students who had a lower level of anxiety tended to score high in school examinations.

Geethanathan P.S. (1998) studied student's moral judgment in relation in relation to certain personal and demographic variables such as locality, sex and class in which studying, and certain psychological variables such as socio-economic status, intellectual ability and attitude towards religion. The sample comprised of thousand four hundred students equally distributed between the two localities. The tools were used to collect the data were Moral Judgment Questionnaire and Raven's Progressive Matrices Test. The major findings were: students of different classes in schools and of different age groups differed significantly in their moral judgment; urban students exhibited higher moral judgment than their rural counterparts; boys and girls did not differ significantly; students of different intellectual abilities differed significantly; and students of different socio-economic strata differed significantly with respect to their moral judgment. Students belonging to different subgroups differed significantly in attitude towards religion in their moral judgment

CONCLUSION

The study of related literature has helped the investigator to have a clear perspective of the problem chosen for the present investigation. The researcher has formulated the hypotheses for the present study. Designing of the method of research / description of the variables, sample selection, selection of suitable tools, administration and scoring methods are being discussed in the succeeding chapter.

❐

3

Research Design and Methodology

Research design is a catalogue of the various phases and facts relating to the formulation of a research effort. It is an arrangement of the essential conditions for collection and analysis of data in a form that aims to combine relevance to research purpose with economy in the procedure.

Every human being is endowed with inner drives. They influence his thoughts, his attitudes, his emotions and his behavior. Religion which is at the same time anubhava (an experience of reality) and darsana (a vision in to reality influences man's behavior much more than any other reality. The sense of 'beyond' which man feels in himself compels him to go in search of it. The metaphysical in our day to day existence.

After gaining adequate theoretical perspective about religious attitude and moral anxiety of Higher secondary school students suitable hypotheses were proposed and appropriate design has been developed to collect the required data to prove the hypotheses statistically.

HYPOTHESES

1. The level of Religious attitude of higher secondary school students is neutral.

2. The level of moral anxiety of higher secondary school students is average in Nature.
3. There is no significant difference between boys and girls of higher secondary schools in their religious attitude.
4. There is no significant difference between students studying in standard XI and XII in their religious attitude.
5. There is no significant difference between students studying in English and Tamil medium of the higher secondary schools in their religious attitude.
6. There is no significant difference between students studying in Government and Private higher secondary schools in their religious attitude.
7. There is no significant difference between boys and girls in the higher secondary schools in the moral anxiety.
8. There is no significant difference between students studying in Standard XI and XII in their moral anxiety.
9. There is no significant difference between students studying in English and Tamil medium of the higher secondary schools in their moral anxiety.
10. There is no significant difference between students studying in Government and Private higher secondary schools in their moral anxiety.
11. There is no significant difference between the religious attitude and moral anxiety among the higher secondary schools students.

RESEARCH TOOLS SELECTED FOR THE PRESENT STUDY

As the present study investigates the religious attitude and moral anxiety Higher secondary school students, the tools taken by the investigator are as follows.

1. Religious attitude scale by Rajamanickam.M.
2. Moral Anxiety scale by Lawrence R.Good and Katherine.C

RELIGIOUS ATTITUDE SCALE

Description

In order to measure attitude towards religion, Rajamanickam's religious attitude scale was used. Religious attitude scale consists of 60 statements pertaining to various aspects of religion. 30 statements are positive and 30 are negative statements. The scorer has to check whether the statement is positive or negative. If positive 1 mark may be entered on the scoring sheet if strongly agree response is underlined. If agree is underlined 2 may be entered, 3 for unable to decide, 4 for disagree and 5 for strongly agree.

If the statement is negative strongly agree response will receive 5, agree 4, unable to decide 3, disagree 2, and strongly disagree 1.

Thus for the whole scale the lowest possible score is 60 which is excrement pro-religious attitude and highest possible score is 300 which in extreme anti-religious attitude.

The individuals score may be sub-divided into six components on the basis of value areas like.

1. Nature of God
2. Prayer and Worship
3. Formal Religion
4. Priests
5. Future life
6. Spirits and Spirit world
7. Administration of Test

The investigator established rapport with the students and explained the purpose of the investigation. The investigator made the students to sit properly in the class. Their responses would be kept confidential in the strict sense. The religious attitude scale was distributed to the students and asked to record their responses by putting a tick mark in the five point scale which is shown below.

They were asked to answer all 60 statements without omission and encouraged to clarify doubts regarding items.

Scoring

If the statement is positive, then the following marks were allotted which is given below.

TABLE. 3.1

Strongly Agree	Agree	Unable to decide	Disagree	Strongly disagree
1	2	3	4	5

If the statement is negative then the following marks were allotted as given below.

TABLE. 3.2

Strongly Agree	Agree	Unable to decide	Disagree	Strongly disagree
5	4	3	2	1

TABLE: 3.3: Scorning Key for Religious Attitude Scalf

Description	Item Number	Strongly Agree	Agree	Unable to decide	Disagree	Strongly disagree
Potitive item	1,2,3,4,5,6,7,8,9,10 11,15,17,19,20,27, 28,29,31,32,33,34,36,3 7,42,46,47,48,50,54,57	1	2	3	4	5
Negative item	3,12,13,14,16,18,21,22 ,23,24,25,26,30,35,38, 39,40,41,43,44,45,49,5 1,52,53,55,56,58,59,60	5	4	3	2	1

TABLE. 3.4: Table Showing Range of Scores and Levels of Attitude

Range of Scores	Level of Attitude
60-90	Extremely pro-religious
91-150	Moderately pro-religious
151-210	Neutral
211-270	Moderately Anti-religious
271-300	Extremely Anti-religious

If the scores fall in between 60 and 90 they are referred to extremely pro-religious attitude, the scores in between 91 and 150 moderately pro-religious, the scores in between 151 and 210 – neutral, the scores in between 211 and 270 moderately anti-religious and the scores in between 271 and 300 extremely anti – religious.

MORAL ANXIETY SCALE

Description

In order to measure the anxiety the anxiety towards morality, Lawrence R.Good and Katherin C.Good scale was used. It consists of 34 statements and each statement can be answered as true or false.

Administration

The investigator established rapport with the students and explained the purpose of the investigation. The investigator made the students to sit properly in the class and informed them to read the statements carefully to decide whether the statements are true or false. The moral anxiety questionnaire was distributed to the students and they were informed to mark in the appropriate space for each statement. They were asked to answer all the 34 statements without omission and encouraged to clarify it necessary.

Scoring

The score for moral anxiety questionnaire is the total number of statements which has been answered 'true'. The score on this questionnaire can range from'0' to '34'.

Interpretation of the Score

As Sigmund Freud stated, some worry about doing what is morally right is necessary in social situations. Such worry helps one to be considered and concerned about others in the society.

Thus a very low level of moral anxiety (a score of 8 or less) may suggest an indifference to the needs of others, a kind of egoism and independence from concern fellow human beings.

At the other end of the continuum, however, a very high level of moral anxiety (scores of 22 or greater) may relate to an inability to relax and enjoy life.

Some one that worried about violating moral principles may adopt a rigid, self-effecting approach life. Worry may take so much energy that there may be little left for actual socially concerned behaviour.

Scores ranging from 9 to 21, the average, suggest a reasonable balance of independent motivation and socially responsible behavior.

TABLE. 3.5: Moral Anxiety Score

Low	Average	Very High Level
8 and less suggest to concern about fellow human beings	9 to 21 Balance of socially Balance of socially responsible behaviour	22 and greater inability to relax and enjoy life.

PILOT STUDY

A Pilot study was conducted among 50 higher secondary school students to establish the reliability and validity of the different tools used in the present study.

ESTABLISHING RELIABILITY AND VALIDITY

The reliability of a test may be defined s the degree of consistency with which, the test measures, what it does measure. The reliability of the tool was calculated using odd even method.

Religious attitude scale

Reliability and Validity

In order to establish the reliability of the religious attitude scale, odd even mean method was used. The reliability of religious attitude scale, was found to be 0.64.

The index of validity which is the square root of reliability was found to be 0.80. The Questionnaire was valid.

Moral anxiety scale

In order to establish the reliability of the moral anxiety scale, odd even method was used. The reliability of moral anxiety sale was found to be 0.66.

The index of validity which is the square root of reliability was found to be .81. The Questionnaire was highly valid.

MAIN STUDY

The tools used for this study are given below:

1. Religious Attitude scale by Rajamanickam.
2. Moral Anxiety sale by Lawrence R.Good and Katherine C.Good.

The above two tools were used for collection of data for the main study with the following procedures followed. After administering the test, the responses were scored using the scoring keys and each students assigned various scores.

SAMPLE FOR THE MAIN STUDY

The investigator in the present study used the stratified random sampling technique. The samples selected for the study were higher secondary school students from Dharmapuri District in Tamil Nadu.

The sample was stratified on the basis of (Gender male and female) the classes (XIth and XIIth standard) The type of school management (Government and Private) and the medium of instruction (English and Tamil medium schools). The size of sample was 300 students, taken from six schools in Dharmapuri District of Tamil Nadu State.

TABLE 3.6: Distribution of the Sample Selected for the Study

S. No.	Name of School	Gender		Class		Medium		Type of Manage-ment		Total
		Male	Female	XI	XII	English	Tamil	Govt.	Private	
1.	Govt. Higher. Secondary School, Lakkiampatti	25	25	25	25	0	50	50	0	50
2.	Senthil Matric Higher Secondary School, Gandhi Nagar	25	25	25	25	50	0	0	50	50
3.	Government Higher Secondary School, Hale Dharmapuri	25	25	25	25	0	50	50	0	50

S. No.	Name of School	Gender		Class		Medium		Type of Management		Total
4.	Vijay Vidhalaya Matric Higher Secondary School, Dharmapuri	0	50	50	0	50	0	0	50	50
5.	Don Bosco Matric Higher Secondary School, Gundalpatty	50	0	50	0	50	0	0	50	50
6.	Government Higher Secondary School, Adhiyamankottai	25	25	25	25	0	50	50	0	50
	Total	**150**	**150**	**200**	**100**	**150**	**150**	**150**	**150**	**300**

STATISTICAL TECHNIQUES USED IN THE MAIN STUDY

Suitable descriptive and inferential statistical techniques were used in the interpretation of the data to draw out a meaningful picture of results from the collected data. In the present study, following statistical techniques were used.

1. Mean
2. Standard Deviation
3. Correlation
4. 't' test
5. Quartile Deviation

CONCLUSION

This chapter outlines the design of the present study, the procedure followed and the nature of the sample. It describes the hypothesis to be tested, the tools to be used and the methods of administration and scoring. The method of investigation designed was found to be quite appropriate and effective for the study. The various statistical techniques were implemented to analyse and systematize the data that were obtained through the test in finding out Religious attitude and moral anxiety among the higher secondary school students. Further, these results were discussed in the light of the hypotheses formulated.

❐

4

Analysis and Interpretation of the Data

"A search design is the arrangements of condition for collection and analysis of data in a manner that aims to combine relevance to the research purpose with economy in procedure"

– Cliare Selltiz (1962).

This chapter highlights the analysis of data obtained to assess the religious attitude and moral anxiety among the higher secondary school students. Using appropriate statistical techniques hypothesis framed for the present study were verified and the findings interpreted and discussed in the light of previous research studies. Hence the present chapter, serves as guide to research, to show how all the major parts of the projects the objectives, the review of literature, hypotheses, and statistical techniques work together to address the Central research questions. At the outset, the following hypothesizes have been formulated keeping in mind the objectives of the present study.

HYPOTHESIS -I

The level of religious attitude of higher secondary school students in neutral in nature.

TABLE. 4.1: Showing the Level of Religion Attiude Among the Higher Secondary School Students.

Variables	Level	Number	Percentage
Religious Attitude	Moderately pro-religious	60	20.00
	Neutral	216	72.00
	Moderately Anti-religious	24	8.00
	Total	**300**	**100.00**

From the above table it is clear that the level of religious attitude among higher secondary school. Students is neutral in nature and the hypothesis is accepted.

HYPOTHESIS II

The level of moral anxiety among the higher secondary school students is average in Nature.

TABLE. 4.2: Showing the Level of Moral Anziety Among the Higher Secondary School Students

Variables	Level	Number	Percentage
Moral Anxiety	Average	172	57.33
	High	128	42.67
	Total	**300**	**100.00**

From the above table it is clear that the level of moral anxiety among the higher secondary school students is average in nature, confirming the Hypothesis.

HYPOTHESIS - III

There is no significant difference between boys and girls of higher secondary school in their religious attitude.

TABLE. 4.3: Significant difference between mean score of Religious Attitude of higher secondary school students based on gender

Variables	Gender	Number	Mean	S.D.	SEMD	C.R. Value	L.S.
Religious attitude	Boys	150	175.60	29.28	2.391	1.92	N.S.
	Girls	150	169.75	23.08	1.885		

From the above table it is clear that there is no significant difference between boys and girls in their religious attitude. Thus the null hypothesis is accepted.

HYPOTHESIS - IV

There is no significant difference between students studying in standard XIth and XIIth in their religious attitude.

TABLE. 4.4: Significant difference between mean score of Religious Attitude of Higher Secondary School Students based on the Standard XIth and XIIth Classes

Variables	Class	Number	Mean	S.D.	SEMD	C.R value	L.S.
Religious attitude	XI	200	172.36	26.93	1.904	0.29	NS
	XII	100	173.30	25.69	2.569		

From the above table it is clear that there is no significant difference between students studying in XI and XII in their religious attitude. So the null hypothesis is accepted.

HYPOTHESIS - V

There is no significant difference between students studying in Tamil and English medium of higher secondary school in their religious attitude.

TABLE. 4.5: Significant difference between mean score of Religious Attitude of Higher Secondary School Students based on Medium of Instruction

Variables	Medium of Instruction	Number	Mean	S.D.	SEMD	C.R. value	L.S.
Religious attitude	English	150	169.34	29.59	2.416	2.20	0.05
	Tamil	150	176.01	22.57	1.843		

From the above table it is clear that there is significant difference between English and Tamil medium higher secondary school students in their religious attitude at .05 level. Thus the null hypothesis is rejected.

HYPOTHESIS - VI

There is no significant difference between students studying in Government and private of higher secondary schools in their religious attitude.

TABLE.4.6: Significant difference between mean score of Religious Attitude of Higher Secondary School Students based on Type of Management

Variables	Type of Management	Number	Mean	S.D.	SEMD	C.R. value	L.S.
Religious attitude	Government	150	176.01	22.575	1.843	2.20	0.05
	Private	150	169.34	29.594	2.416		

From the above table it is clear that there is a significant difference between Government and private higher secondary school students in their religious attitude at .05 level. Thus the null hypothesis is rejected.

HYPOTHESIS - VII

There is no significant difference between boys and girls in the higher secondary schools in the moral anxiety.

TABLE. 4.7: Significant difference between mean score of Moral Anxiety of Higher Secondary School Students based on Gender

Variables	Medium of Instruction	Number	Mean	S.D.	SEMD	C.R value	L.S.
Moral Anxiety	Boys	150	21.06	5.794	.473	0.76	N.S.
	Girls	150	20.55	5.907	.482		

From the above table it is clear that there is a significant difference between boys and girls in their Moral anxiety. Therefore the null hypothesis is accepted.

HYPOTHESIS - VIII

There is no significant difference between students studying in standard XIth and XIIth in their moral anxiety.

TABLE. 4.8: Significant difference between mean score of Moral Anxiety of Higher Secondary School Students based on the Standard XIth and XIIth Classes

Variables	Class	Number	Mean	S.D.	SEMD	C.R. value	L.S.
Moral Anxiety	XI	200	21.58	5.618	.397	3.30	0.01
	XII	100	19.26	6.013	.601		

From the above table it is clear that there is a significant difference between students studying std XIth and XIIth in their Moral anxiety at .01 level. The null hypothesis is rejected based on the level of significance.

HYPOTHESIS - IX

There is no significant difference between students studying in English and Tamil medium of the higher secondary schools in their moral anxiety.

TABLE 4.9: Significant difference between mean score of Moral Anxiety of Higher Secondary School Students based on Medium of Instruction

Variables	Medium of instruction	Number	Mean	S.D.	SEMD	C.R. value	L.S.
Moral Anxiety	English	150	22.46	5.230	.427	5.11	0.01
	Tamil	150	19.15	5.976	.488		

From the above table it is clear that there is a significant difference between English and Tamil medium higher secondary school students in their moral anxiety at 0.01 level. Therefore the null hypothesis is rejected.

HYPOTHESIS - X

There is no significant difference between students studying in Government and Private Secondary schools in their moral anxiety.

TABLE. 4.10: Significant difference between mean score of Moral Anxiety of Higher Secondary School Students based on Type of Management

Variables	Type of Management	Number	Mean	S.D.	SEMD	C.R. value	L.S.
Moral Anxiety	Government	150	19.15	5.976	.488	5.11	0.01
	Private	150	22.46	5.230	.427		

From the above table it is clear that there is a significant difference between Government and Private higher secondary school students in their Moral Anxiety at .01 level. Thus the null hypothesis is rejected.

HYPOTHESIS - XI

There is no significant relationship among Religious attitude and moral anxiety.

TABLE. 4.11: Showing the correlation among Religion Attitude and Moral Anxiety

Variables	Number of Students	Correlation	L.S.
Religious attitude	300	0.04	N.S.
Moral anxiety			

From the above table it is clear that there is no significant relationship among Religious attitude and moral anxiety. Therefore, the above hypothesis is rejected.

CONCLUSION

The analysis and interpretation of data reveals that there is no significant association between Religious attitude and moral anxiety among the higher secondary school students. The religious attitude of the higher secondary school students is found to be the neutral category. The majority of the high secondary school. Students fall in the average group with regard to moral anxiety. The next chapter deals with the major findings and summary of the study.

❐

5

Summary and Findings

The investigation was an attempt to study the religious attitude and moral anxiety of the higher secondary school students. Apart from this students attitude to various aspects of religion such as nature of God, Prayer and Worship, Formal Religion, Priests, Future Life, Spirit and Spirit world were also investigated on the basis of Sex, religious affiliation, gender type of management, classes and medium of instruction.

It is observed that there is no relationship between religious attitude and moral anxiety of the higher secondary school students. It is assumed that people's religious attitude may go with moral anxiety. The objectives and hypothesis the methodology and the major findings are presented.

In this study the sample of be 300 students from higher secondary schools in Dharmapuri District were tested using Religious attitude scale and moral anxiety. the information were collected, the data were statistically treated, analyzed, interpreted, discussed and concluded.

STATEMENT OF THE STUDY

The present investigation is titled as, "Religious attitude and Moral anxiety of higher secondary school students.

OBJECTIVES OF THE STUDY

1. To find out the level of Religious attitude of higher secondary school students.
2. To find out the level of Moral Anxiety of higher secondary school students.

3. To find out the significant difference between boys and girls of higher secondary school in their religious attitude.
4. To find out the significant difference between students studying in standard XIth and XIIth in their religious attitude.
5. To find out the significant difference between students studying in English and Tamil medium of the higher secondary schools in their religious attitude.
6. To find out the significant difference between students studying in Government and Private higher secondary schools in their religious attitude.
7. To find out the significant difference between boys and girls of higher secondary schools in their moral anxiety.
8. To find out the significant difference between students studying in standard XIth and XIIth in their moral anxiety.
9. To find out the significant difference between student studying in English and Tamil medium of the higher secondary schools in their moral anxiety.
10. To find out the significant difference between students studying in Government and Private higher secondary school in their moral anxiety.
11. To find out the relationship between religious attitude and moral anxiety of higher secondary school students.

HYPOTHESES OF THE STUDY

1. The level of Religious attitude of higher secondary school students is neutral.
2. The level of moral anxiety of higher secondary school students is average in Nature.
3. There is no significant difference between boys and girls of higher secondary schools in their religious attitude.
4. There is no significant difference between students studying in standard XIth and XIIth in their religious attitude.
5. There is no significant difference between students studying in English and Tamil medium of the higher secondary schools in their religious attitude.
6. There is no significant difference between students studying in Government and Private higher secondary schools in their religious attitude.
7. There is no significant difference between boys and girls in the higher secondary schools in the moral anxiety.
8. There is no significant difference between students studying in Standard XIth and XIIth in their moral anxiety.

9. There is no significant difference between students studying in English and Tamil medium of the higher secondary schools in their moral anxiety.
10. There is no significant difference between students studying in Government and Private higher secondary schools in their moral anxiety.
11. There is no significant relationship among the religious attitude and moral anxiety of students in the higher secondary schools.

SAMPLE OF THE STUDY

The sample population consisted of 300 higher secondary school students studying in Government and Private schools in Tamil Nadu. Six schools from the Dharmapuri District of Tamil Nadu have been chosen randomly for the study. Out of the sample of 300 students, 150 are male students and 150 are female students.

MAJOR FINDINGS OF THE STUDY

1. The major findings have been arrived at the present investigation are as follows:
2. It was found that the level of religious attitude among higher secondary school students is neutral in nature.
3. It was found that the level of moral anxiety among higher secondary school students is average in nature.
4. It was found that there is no significant difference between boys and girls in relation to their religious attitude.
5. It was found that there is no significant difference between students studying in standard XIth and XIIth in their religious attitude.
6. It was found that there is significant difference between English and Tamil medium higher secondary school students in their religious attitude
7. It was found that there is significant difference between Government and Private higher secondary school students in their religious attitude.
8. It was found that there is no significant difference between boys and girls in their moral anxiety.
9. It was found that there is a significant difference between students studying in standard XIth and XIIth in their moral anxiety.
10. It was found that there is a significant difference between English and Tamil medium higher secondary school students in their moral anxiety.
11. It was found that there is a significant difference between Government and Private higher secondary school students in their moral anxiety.

12. It was found that there is no significant relationship among Religious attitude and moral anxiety.

EDUCATION IMPLICATIONS

The aim of education is to develop abroad mindedness and universal outlook in the students with the right wisdom. This study would provide a chance for the students to be more religious and moral oriented some schools it appears that there is no systematic religious or moral instruction given to students. The religious practices were carried out at the homes of the students in most cases. It appears that such students are not having any strong view about the nature of god and religious principles.

The education system must impart values in students such as tolerance, patience, understanding, truthfulness, gratitude faith in God, self respect and also in the education at should raise it perspective the humanity and acquire the value of brotherhood, mercy, love etc.

The study also observes that the students do not have sufficient knowledge about any aspect of the religion they believe. When they grow old the same attitude to religion is carried by them, thus resulting in lack of building moral values and religious faith.

Morality is the beginning for into any religious group. At the same time by religious path one can enter in the goal of spiritual attainment. So, education should give clarity to the students about the need for moral values, and religious faith. Education should provide a proper understanding about every individual's life goal in relation to material and spiritual aspects.

Well-conducted classes on Religious or moral institutions could help students to become tolerant and respectful towards others. The school could organize sports events, cultural events and exhibitions encouraging students participation which would further improve development of values, provision and opportunities for students to work in collaboration with one another and to enhance religious tolerance.

Finally, education can only provide the right understanding in life to balance the religious and moral aspects concerning an individual.

SUGGESTIONS FOR FURTHER RESEARCH

Some suggestions with regard to possibilities of the research in the field of education are offered with a view to stimulate prospective research workers in this area.

1. The influence of institutions like home, school and political ideologies upon the religious attitude of the students.
2. Religious attitude in relation to personality traits such as introvertism and extrovertism.

3. The present study is limited to Government and private higher secondary school students and it could be extended to the University Level Students.
4. A similar study may be undertaken in other states of Tamil Nadu.

CONCLUSION

Good citizens contribute to the primary aims of education to bring about a change and get then to be realized and envisaged in the long run.

Moral anxiety is a progressive and positive level in the human life towards attaining spiritual development.

Education also provides opportunity to raise subjective moral questions regarding behaviour of their own self or others. Such type of introspective questions and moral anxiety in behaviour is seen in students, especially at the adolescent period. Encouraged by the life of their teachers and the religious living atmosphere at home and the parents, they may be morally anxious and their gives rise to the concept of religious attitude which can be closely linked to the moral anxiety of individuals.

❐

6

The Problem and its Perspectivies

Socialization is the process by which a person develops from a mere biological organism, as at birth to an adequate adult human person. Socialization means learning the ways of a culture. No human is regarded as fully-growth until learns to display a measure of the prevailing adult attitudes, values, beliefs and knowledge of the subculture to which he belongs.

Socialization requires moving through a series of age-related subcultures. At any given time in the life of a growing child or youth we may refer to the dominant thought patterns of his age mates as his peer culture. This statement should be qualified with the observation that until a child is old enough to become a member of neighborhood playgroup, or a nursery school group, he has no true peer culture. During the first two or three years of life the only culture he knows is that part of the adult culture which his parents and adult relatives teach him, or the peer culture which older siblings transmit.

The nature of peer culture changes continuously as children grow older. For any given age level, the peer culture changes with the passage of time. This change is very conspicuous, for example, in the case of teen-age jargon and teen-age clothing, eating, and dating habits. Adults rarely understand child and youth peer culture. They see the surface of it, but with childish wisdom youngsters realize that it saves trouble to keep a part of the peer culture hidden from adult view.

Man is aware of himself. He can think of himself. Biologically self-awareness is an evolutionary novelty. So the problem is how the neonate who has no awareness whatever develops into an adult with self-awareness.

Defining the Family

Families are defined as special variants of intimate relationship systems for which the maintenance of boundaries, privacy, closeness, and permanence are crucial, albeit empirically more or less variable, defining elements. This definition not only includes nontraditional family forms found in modern society but also focuses on a genuine psychological perspective; that is, how and to what extent people influence each other and are influenced by the relationship context in which they are living. In addition, it takes into account the dynamic nature of the co-developing individual-family unit by explicitly considering the possibility that a person might be part of a series of quite different intimate relationship system across his or her life course.

The Family and Health

There is ample evidence that people living in a long-term (usually marital) relationship are, on average, physically and psychologically healthier than single, divorced, or widowed person. For instance, the data suggest that in the United States the death rates of unmarried people are up to 50 percent (females) or even 25 percent (males) higher than for married people. Causes of death with a strong behavioral component (e.g., lung cancer, suicide, accidents) have a particularly high incidence rate for unmarried people. Moreover, clinically diagnosed personality dysfunctions (e.g., anxiety, depression) are also more likely to be found among this group.

Family Violence

In some cases the family itself may became a health risk. In Western societies this is especially true for children and women, increasingly also for older family members, whose personal integrity can be violated by physical maltreatment and sexual abuse. The expression and definition of domestic violence is different from country to country; the same holds true for corresponding laws, criminal statistics, and estimated numbers of unknown cases. Despite these differences, there is consistent evidence that domestic violence is rapidly increasing in the Western industrialized nations, quite apart from the growing neglect of children in economically deprived Third World countries. The causes and consequences of family violence and neglect are in general well-researched, suggesting a multidimensional pattern of causes among which variables like economic hardship, social and personal stress, low self-esteem, unrealistic expectations of child-rearing, and a history of experience of violence in one's own family of origin are especially salient. Several reviews concerning the consequences of child maltreatment lead to similar conclusions; that is, maltreated children tend to be more aggressive, show more internalizing and externalizing behavior problems, are less empathetic, have more troubled peer relationships, and perform lower on cognitive tasks. Preventive action seems to be imperative in view of these findings, although so far the results of corresponding programs have yielded mixed results (Gilles and Conte 1990).

Family Relations

The number of possible relationship within a family increases exponentially with the number of individual family members. In a four-person family, for example, there are 11 groupings of family members. In addition, relations among relationship (e.g., between the couple and the parent-child system) must be taken into account, not to mention the relationships connecting the family and its sub-systems with other social units (e.g., extended family, peers). These complex patterns of relationships should be kept in mind as some of the major types of relationships within the family are briefly reviewed.

Parent-Child Relations

The care and socialization of children are among the most important societal tasks that, to a great extent, are entrusted to the family. Theoretical models to explore the determinants, concomitants and consequences of parenthood have increasingly become more complex by addressing not only specific parent child interactions, but also by looking at contextual and systemic influences such as heredity, child temperament, the parents' personality and relationship history, couple relationship, workplace, social support and economic resources. In addition, theoretical advances, especially using attachment and social-learning approaches, have shown some convergence concerning the development of competent behavior in children and adolescents.

Sibling Relations

Despite declining birthrates in industrialized countries, the sibling relationship still contributes substantially to the process of individual and family development. Beside the more structural properties of sibling constellations (i.e., spacing, distribution of sexes) and their impact on intra and extra familial relationships, more fine-grained behavioral analyses have shown that differential parental treatment is strongly related to the quality of sibling relationships. Siblings who are treated differently by their parents tend to develop poorer and more confliction relationships among themselves and also show more adaptation problems as adolescents (Dunn and Stocker 1989). This might impede the fulfillment of developmental tasks across the sibling life-cycle (e.g., caring for elderly parents, mutual support with health and financial problems). Although siblings tend to develop a closer and less competitive relationship in later life, much more knowledge is required about differential developmental paths of sibilingship in a lifespan perspective.

Intergenerational Relations

With increasing life expectancies, it is becoming more probable that three or even four generations coexist. Relationships between grandparents or great-grand parent and their grandchildren or great-grand children are usually perceived as being rather positive by both sides. Again, differential effects seem to moderate these relationships suggesting specific systematic influences. Thus, it has been shown that, on average, grandchildren report a close relationship with their grandparents only if they also feel that the relationship between their parents and grandparents is emotionally satisfying.

However, intergenerational relations can also be less rewarding and even harmful. The experience of family violence and divorce, for example, seems to have a strong component that is transmitted from generation to generation. The work by Elder et al. (1984) is especially revealing as to the mechanisms of this intergenerational transmission process. By linking the life courses of four generations, these authors were able to demonstrate that insensitive, controlling, and hostile parenting behavior has a detrimental impact on the personality and marital relations of the offspring, which in turn leads to inadequate parenting on their part when they have children of their own. In the same vein, Ratter's (1988) work comparing the parenting behavior of home-reared and institution-reared mothers, showed that mothers who, as children, had to be placed into an institution because of their parents' severe marital discord displayed much poorer parenting, especially if the placement happened before their fourth birthday. These results accord well with increasing research evidence stemming from an attachment theoretical approach. Nevertheless, it should be noted that there are also internal and external resources (e.g., strong personal interests, support from relatives, friends or spouses) that serve as protective factors in coping with adverse life conditions.

Family Therapy

Family therapy is not a monolithic treatment approach. Rather there are many different models and schools expanding almost all theoretical approaches that have been used in individual therapy by adding a systematic or relationship component to the core belief system. For family therapy in its narrower sense, it is indispensable to use sound diagnostic assessment of clinically relevant individual and familial dysfunctions on which family treatment can be based. Depending on the preferred theoretical orientation, research evidence on effective treatment outcomes is still scarce, although in some comparative studies it was shown that family therapy was equal or even superior to other treatment approaches.

The responsibilities of the Family

Family is very important because from it he inherits the cultural traditions. From this viewpoint family becomes more important for man. It is generally seen that if one is deprived of family protection, his development remains incomplete. Therefore for the desirable development of the child the family has to hold certain responsibilities.

The child's first education begins in the family. The making or unmaking of his future life depends on his early experiences in the family. The mother influences the child immensely. After the mother, the father and sisters and brothers, guests, servants and casual visitors leave their impact on the child. The child has an inherent power to receive education consciously or unconsciously from the various aspects of his environment. Because of this conscious or unconscious learning the child is rightly regarded as the symbol of the interest, traditions, ideals and culture of his family. Thus when he comes to the school, he brings with his personality the traditions and culture of his family.

Many families in our country are not able to maintain a desirable atmosphere for development of children. In some families it is due to poor economic conditions or due to lack of unity and emotional bond, and in some it is due to lack of necessary knowledge on the part of parents, some families are able to provide good environment. In such families the children are always encouraged to strive in various good directions.

The parents have to understand the specific interests, aptitudes and capacities of children particularly when they reach the puberty stage. The child must not be encouraged to prepare itself for a particular vocation. Nothing has to be imposed on him. If he does not want to prepare himself for medical profession, he must not be pressed for the same. If he himself expressed a desire for civil engineering, he may be allowed to go ahead as he wants.

A child has an acute sense of curiosity. For fulfilling the same he is never tired of putting questions to the elders in the family. His questions must be answered in an appropriate manner and he must never be scolded for the style and contents of his questions. We must remember that the child is just in the process of growth.

Since a decade or so, the tendency in most of the schools is seen that the school teachers leave enough for the parents as regards teaching of children. At the time of admission the parents are also interviewed along with children. This implies that the school is now drifting towards a direction in which the responsibilities of parents with regard to education of children are being gradually increased. Therefore, the parents have now to devote sometime daily to the education of children. They must see that children do the assigned home work rightly without fail. Besides, the parents must also teach the children that which they could not follow in the school. Thus we find that the responsibility of the family with regard to education of children is being gradually widened. So no parents should feel complacent about education of their wards. Either the father or mother has to perform this duty every day. Thus the parents must not feel satisfied about the education f their children just by procuring admission for them in some good school. The situation was not so three decades ago. Evidently, the responsibilities of the family have been multiplied manifold for education of children. The family must fulfill these responsibilities in co-operation with the school.

PEER GROUP RELATIONSHIP

Peer Groups

These are groups in which most members are of equal age and of similar social status. People of all age levels form peer groups of their own. However, here, peer groups among children and youth are considered. While the world of the very young child is largely that of the parents and the home, older children and youth love in the dual world of their peer and adults. While a child at the primary school level is strongly family-oriented, the high school student is much more influenced by his peer group. Boys are much more peer oriented than girls in the high school stage, and get free from the influence of their families, with regard to their opinions and attitudes. Peer group influences are encouraged by extra curricular activities, sports and other social influences. Peer groups develop certain status symbols, which change from time to time. A status symbol establishes communication and relationship between peer group members; for example, long hair, blue jeans, striped shirts, and other fashions may become “the rage” for a while.

Functions of Peer Groups

Peer groups are important to the young, in the development of the self and also in the learning of cultures. They help the young to become independent in their thoughts and decisions. Peer groups during adolescence are very significant, especially in western cultures. Such developmental tasks as learning to get along with companions and acquire a satisfactory sex role can be adequately achieved only through satisfactory peer relationships. Many of the attitudes of the teen-ager are a result of group influence and stimulation. The peer group represents a distinctive sub-culture in contemporary western society and even in Indian society to a lesser degree.

The peer group is primarily an activity group, which operates through social, recreational and vocational activities. The peer group provides sex-education in many cases. It assists the individual teen-ager in the process of self-identification and self-discovery. Social and emotional emancipation from the family is possible through the peer group. He acquires a status, which he cannot get in adult society. Thus the adolescent's personality develops through the important social agency known as "the peer group".

Importance of Peer Relationships

During adolescence the need to belong to and identify with a group of individuals of the same age is stronger than it is at any other period. This tendency seems to hold in most contemporary societies. Adolescents spend a great deal of time with their own age-group, and the values and attitudes of their own particular set of friends within the peer-group become an important influence on their behavior. The reasons for the growing importance of peer relationships are varied but three major areas can be distinguished.

1. To begin with, relations"with both same-and opposite-sex peers serve as prototypes (first examples) of adult social relationships. Adolescence is a period in which learning about interpersonal behavior in a variety of situations-social, intimate, and work-oriented-speeds up and, as you will know from your own experience, even a short period of a year or eighteen months can produce a striking change in the social, intimate, and work-oriented-speeds up and, as you will know from your own experience, even a short period of a year or eighteen months can produce a striking change in the social maturity of the adolescent. Much of this social maturity is acquired in interactions with peers.
2. Another reason for the increasing dependence on peers lies in the fact that "ties with adults loosen as children grow older". For a number of reasons many parents are not able to revive their own memories of the emotions and changes of adolescence and so adolescents seek others of the same age-group to share their doubts and uncertainties about the future and their defeats and victories of the present, This is not to say that, as we discussed before and shall return to later, there are necessarily conflicts of values between adults and peers, but merely that other peers have more time, inclination and patience to share the often introspective thoughts that are characteristic of adolescence.
3. Peers also help the adolescent in defining his sense of himself. No longer a child, not yet an adult, the adolescent must prepare to meet the demands his society makes of adult functioning in many spheres-social, sexual and vocational. The peer-group, members of which are

facing similar choices, can help the adolescent in defining his sense of self and his expectations of the future.

Peer Relations and Development

A peer system refers to the interactions, relationships and group structures involving persons in a group of nearly the same developmental level. Age level is often used as an indicator for peer status. However, in many instances age mates are not peers. For example, in most school achievement domains mentally retarded persons are not peers of intellectually normal individuals. Furthermore, age mates may not be peers in every developmental domain. In athletics physically handicapped persons are not peers of non-handicapped individuals, although they may be peers in intellectual competence. Class group are often homogeneous on a number of characteristics, such as age level, achievement level, learning difficulties, and so on. the goal of this entry is to describe the relevance of peer relations in school classes for children's social, emotional, and personality development.

Peer competence and the Peer System

In a conceptual framework for the understanding of social relationships in groups, Hinder (1976) has distinguished three hierarchic levels: Interactions between individuals are seen as basic elements for social relationships. Relationships are the basis for group structure. Description of an interaction requires specification of the content, that is, what individuals are doing together (e.g., A does X to B and B responds with Y), and the equality of an interaction. An essential aspect of the quality of an interaction is its valence. Whether an interaction is positive/prosaically or negative/antisocial is an important determinant of the meaning of an interaction for a relationship.

Goniometric Status, Peer Competence, and Developmental Pathways

In a meta-analysis of 41 studies, Newcomb et al. (1993) investigated goniometric group differences on several aspects of aggression, sociability, withdrawal, and academic/intellectual ability. Information was moderately consistent over four different sources: observation, and peer, adult, and self reports. Popular children are most liked by peers and best friends, and show higher levels of sociability and cognitive abilities and lower levels of aggression and withdrawal. They have the social abilities to achieve interpersonal goals and to maintain positive relationships. Although popular children are able to be assertive/aggressive, their behavioral repertoire primarily leads to positive social outcomes for themselves and for others and they score low on measures of general aggression, negative affect, and disruption. Rejected children provide a nearly polar opposite to the behavior patterns of popular children. They are more aggressive and withdrawn and less sociable and cognitively skilled than average children. In contrast to controversial children, who have the highest level of aggressive behavior, rejected children lack positive qualities that balance out their aggressive behavior rejected children are at risk in their social development.

Intervention and Treatment Programs

Numerous treatment programs have been developed, although most of them have been limited in scope and in time, in theoretical background, and in setting. For example, specific behavioral or social-cognitive responses have been trained during a few weeks or months outside the class or home in child-focused approaches. Although such programs have often been effective, they do not provide adequate long-term maintenance of improvement. Peer problems often have functional meaning for children and are not restricted to a single setting of school, home or peer group. A child who is aggressive toward peers is often also aggressive at home and toward teachers. Treatments are only effective when they use multiple methods, aim at clearly specified but broad behavioral domains, and are maintained across settings for a long period of time. Therefore, the introduction of treatment programs in schools requires extensive preparation.

Peer Relations and Learning

Children's communication with their peers has qualities that differ from the qualities of adult-child communication. For example, peer dialogues are usually more equal than conversations between adult and child: children usually listen more respectfully to adults than to peers for information and guidance. Such differences have serious implications for learning. Educators have become aware of these differences and have begun to design classroom strategies that best exploit the learning opportunities provided by both peer and adult-child relations. This entry discusses contemporary methods for applying the special features of children's peer relations to their academic learning.

Three Types of Peer Learning

Although peer relations are generally more equal than adult-child relations, not all peer engagements are strictly alike. Peer relations themselves can be unequal to various extents. There are three main types of peer learning that have been introduced into classrooms by educational researchers. These have been called "peer tutoring," "cooperative learning," and "peer collaboration" (Damon and Phelps 1989). As in the contrast between adult-child and peer relations, the three district forms of peer learning offer different strengths and weakness for the educator.

Cooperative Learning

Cooperative learning, also called "small group learning" or "group work", has been introduced into many schools because the available methods are relatively easy for teachers to adopt. The techniques can be integrated into the normal school day without disruptions in the regular classroom routine. Some cooperative learning programs require as little as an hour or two a week of classroom time.

There are a variety of cooperative learning techniques now in use. All begin by dividing classrooms into small "teams" of no more than four or five children. These teams are generally heterogeneous with respect to students' abilities. The teacher presents a task to the team, and the team sets out to master it. All cooperative learning methods rely on team solidarity and the motivation that it engenders. The assumption is that students will want to perform well for their team and that they will work for the success of their fellow team members and the team as a whole.

Peer Tutoring

In this approach, a child trains another child in skills and subject matter that the first child has mastered. Because the first child has greater information or competence than the second child, the two do not begin the relationship with equal status: rather, the first child is considered an expert and the second child a relative novice. Moreover, the unequal status of the two children is often compounded by other factors as well. Most attempts at peer tutoring pair an older child with a younger child, or a bright child with an educationally disadvantaged one. Peer tutoring, in fact, is often called "cross-age" tutoring, since the tutor is usually two or more years older than the tutee.

Peer Collaboration

In peer collaboration, a pair of novices works together to solve difficult tasks. This method differs from peer tutoring because the children begin at roughly the same levels of competence. It also differs from cooperative learning, because children work jointly on the same problem rather than individually on separate components of the problem. In actual practice, however, peer collaboration bears some resemblance to other types of peer learning. Even in peer collaboration, one child may assume the lead spontaneously; and the collaborators may separate for independent work.

Statement of the Problem

"Family and Peer Relationship among high school students.

OPERATIONAL DEFINITION

Family Relation

According to the view of the investigator the term family relation refers to the scores obtained from the family relations index contracted and standardized by Walter W.Hudson

Peer Relation

According to the view of the investigator the term family relation refers to the scores obtained from the Peer relations index contracted and standardized by Walter W.Hudson

High School Students

By this the investigator means that the students studying in ninth and tenth Standard.

Objectives of the Study

1. To find out the Level of Family Relation among High School Students.
2. To find out the Level of Peer Relation among High School Students.
3. To find out the significant difference between male and female High Students on their Family Relation.
4. To find out the significant difference between male and female High School Students on their Peer Relation.
5. To find out the significant difference between high school student from nuclear and Joint family on their Family Relation
6. To find out the significant difference between high school student from nuclear and Joint family on their Peer Relation.
7. To find out the significant difference between rural and urban high school students on their family relations.
8. To find out the significant difference between rural and urban high school students on their peer relation.
9. To find out the significant difference between Tamil and English medium high school students on their family relation
10. To find out the signification difference between Tamil and English medium high school students on their peer relation.
11. To find out the significant difference among High School students of different age groups on their family relation.
12. To find out the significant difference among High School Students of different age groups on their Peer Relation.
13. To find out the significant difference among High School Students of different type of management on their Family Relation.

14. To find out the significant difference among High School Students from different Type of management on their Peer Relation.
15. To find out the significant different among High School Students of different Parental Qualification in their Family Relation.
16. To find out the significant difference among High School Students of different Parental Qualification in their Peer Relation.
17. To find out the significant difference among high school students of different family income on their Family Relation.
18. To find out the significant difference among high school students of different family income on their Peer Relation.
19. To find out the significant relationship between Family Relation and Peer Relation of high school student.

Limitation

Due to the lack of time the investigator could not study all students studying in and Thiruvannamalai district. The investigator chooses only a simple of three hundred students. The area of the study is limited only Thiruvannamalai educational district. Moreover this study limited only the students studying 9th and 10th Standard.

Summary

In this chapter an overview of the problem, objectives and limitation were discussed. The next chapter deals with the review of related literature related to the problem.

❒

7

Review of Related Literature

The survey of related studies implies locating, studying and evaluating reports of relevant researches, study of published articles, going through related portions of Encyclopedias and research abstracts, study of pertinent pages out of comprehensive books on the subject and going through related manuscripts if any. For any worth while study in any field of knowledge the research worker needs and adequate familiarity with the work which has already been done in the area of his choice. He needs to acquire up-to-date information about what has been thought and done in the particular area. He has to build upon the accumulated and recorded knowledge of the past. He drawn maximum benefit from the previous investigations, utilizes the previous findings, takes many hints from the designs and procedures of previous researches, matches his conclusions with the conclusions drawn earlier and tries to add from his side a line or two the existing store of knowledge.

Purpose the Review of Literature

1. Review of the related literature, besides, allowing the researcher to acquaint him with current knowledge in the field or area in which he is going to conduct his research, serves the following specific purposes:
2. The review of related literature enables the researcher to define the limits of his field. It helps the researcher to delimit and define his problem. The knowledge of related literature, brings the researcher up-to-date on the work which others have done and thus to state the objectives clearly and concisely.

3. By reviewing the related literature the researcher can avoid unfruitful and useless problem areas. He can select those areas in which positive findings are very likely to result and his endeavors would be likely to add to the knowledge in a meaningful way.
4. Through the review of related literature, the researcher can avoid unintentional duplication of well-established findings. It is no use to replicate a study when the stability and validity of its result have been clearly established.
5. The review of related literature gives to researcher an understanding of the research methodology, which refers to the way the study, is to be conducted. It helps the researcher to know about the tools and instruments, which proved to be useful and promising in the previous studies. The advantage of the related literature is also to provide insight into the statistical method through which validity of results is to be established.
6. The final and important specific reason for reviewing the related literature is to know about the recommendations of previous researchers listed in their studies for further research.

Studies Related to Family Relationship:

INDIAN STUDIES

Jain Shikha (1991), conducted a study on child rearing practices, adolescence, cognitive ability and achievement. Students from VII, IX and X class, about 108 in number along with their mothers were interviewed. It was found that, parent who is consistent in disciplining the child was the factor, which positively and significantly related with academic achievement. Further if the child is brought up in a restrictive home environment. It acts as a block towards the academic achievement.

Manual Bheema (1988), made a study on the impact of emotional maturity and prolonged deprivation on indiscipline behavior among students in relation to their achievement. From the sample of 472 students it was found that emotion instability was due to home environment. Child rearing experience and interaction with parents are positively related to academic achievement.

Deb Modha Grewal and Hindai Pal 1990), nvestigated the relationship bgtween study habits and academic achievement of under graduate home science final year students. The study was conducted on asample of 90 students. It was observed that family environment of the students is significantlyrelated to academic achievement.

Deb Modha Grewal and Hindai Pal 1990), nvestigated the relationship bgtween study habits and academic achievement of under graduate home science final year students. The study was conducted on a sample of 90 students. It was observed that family environment of the students is significantly related to academic achievement.

Chandy and Sumi (1991), Conducted a study on application of certain pupil deficit models to differential achievement in English in University of Lateral. About 1040, (538 boys and 507 girls) from 74 schools. The results show that positive family relations improve academic achievement of the students.

Arora Relta (1988), Carried out studies on parent child relationship, teacher – student relationship and achievement of higher secondary students. In his study it was said that there is no significant relationship between achievement and parent child relationship. Educational standards of teacher student relationship were significantly related. Parent child relationship and teacher student relationship are significantly related.

Padhi (1989), studied problem of home environment, the parent child relationship and children's competence during adolescence. About 100 students from classes VII, IX and X formed the sample of study. Among them 50 were girls and 50 were boys. It was found that children with positive self-concept were found to be confident about positive perceptions of their peers and teachers. With regard to the children's peer-checked competence, it was found that parental withdrawal mediated the Childs peer affiliation and indirectly helped to develop the child's competence and self-reliance.

Shah, B. (1989), investigated the effect of family climate on home adjustment of adolescent. The students of class IX of Narwhal Manual constitution were drawn randomly from 12 schools in two districts. The findings say that home adjustment of students having satisfactory family climate was found to be superior to that of those who had highly dissatisfactory family climate. But in the case of girls, family climate did not play an important role in determining the level of home adjustment.

Shukla k. (1992), undertook a study to examine, whether parental behavior and interaction influence the development of social competence of the children. On the basis of income, professional affiliation and material possession about 150 families from high SES and 150 families from low SES were selected. In addition, there being one son and one daughter in the age range 10-15 years in each family was considered. About 30 parentless boys in the above age range from the local orphanage were also part of this sample. Parental authority as well as peer interaction did reveal highly significant main effects on social competence. Both sons and daughters of the upper SES group were found to differ significantly compared to lower SES groups.

Esterman K.And Hedlund D. (1995), studied the comparing Rural Adolescents from Farm and non form families. Interview with 87 adolescents from farm and non-farm. Families in rural New York reveled that farm adolescents were closer to their families, were more isolated from peers and peer-related activities, were less likely to pursue a college degree, and were unlikely to remain on the farm despite the positive aspects of farm life. Address implication for rural education.

Diana (1993), studied the fostering as seen by the careers children. Examined attitudes about foster care of 75 birth children of foster parents. Found that most enjoy or at least tolerate being part of foster family, with many indicating that, despite the problems, it can give them a greater appreciation of their own family and an awareness of the difficulties some of their peers must cope with.

Hoffmann J.P.(1994) studied the Investigating the Age Effects of Family structure on Adolescent Marijuana use. Differences among younger and older adolescents in the influence of family structure, family relations, and peer relation on marijuana use were studied in the sample (n=1,725) from the National Youth Survey, 1976-78. Relative effects of drug-using peers and family variables are identified for younger and older adolescents.

Smith D.E. (1994), studied the relationship between Jamaican Adolescents Drinking Partners and self-image Examined relationship between drinking partner (adult versus peer) and self-image of Jamaican adolescents (n=176) who reported alcohol use. Found that adolescents who drank with adults had significantly higher self-evaluations, reported less emotional fluctuation, had better family relationship, had higher vocational/educational goals, were more socially conscious, and had better psychological adjustment.

Giordano P.C. (1993) studied the Family and Peer Relations of Black Adolescents. Hypothesized that, compared to white adolescents, African – American adolescents maintain more intimate stance toward family, whereas friendships are less intense, and that African Americans perceive lower levels of peer pressure and are more tolerant of behavioral differences in friendships. Data from personal interviews with 942 adolescents lend support to this alternative portrait.

Bullock J.R. (1993) studied the children's loneliness and their relationships with family children's feeling of loneliness related to family and researchers have only recently documented peer relationships. These feelings are now being recognized, researched, and assessed in children as young as five years of age. Helping professionals need to understand short-and long-term consequences of children's loneliness as it relates to their personal well-being and self-esteem.

Yamgblade L.M. And Belsky J. (1992) examined the links between children's relationship with their parents at one and three years and their relationships with a friend at five years. Positive and secure parent-child relationships were associated with childrens positive friendship and negative family relationship with negative friendships several counterintuitive findings emerged.

Freckhall P. And Luks A. (1992), studied the An Evaluation of parental Assessment of the Big Brothers/Big sisters Program in New York city. Parents rated impact of Big Brother/Big Sister Program on children along variables of school attendance, grades, family relationship, friendship, self-esteem, staying out of trouble, being responsible, frequency of contact, and length of time in program. Although children were rated as benefiting significantly from program, children's frequency of contact did not have significant effect on outcome measures.

Windle M. (1992) studied the A Longitudinal, study of stress buffering for Adolescent Problem Behaviors. In a study of middle adolescents, the interrelationships between stressful events, perceived social support, internalization of problems, and externalization of problems were examined. Social support did not act as a buffer of stress. Stressful events and low family support predicted problem behaviors for adolescent girls.

Richarddson R.A. (1991), studied the Informal social network as sources of support and Interference for adolescent mothers. Administered Inventory of social contacts to 46 adolescent mothers to assess perceptions of both support and interference derived from family and peer. Results indicated that, although subject divided considerable support from their networks they also experienced interference from those same individuals. Most significant interference was from relatives in areas of child rearing and emotional/personal concern.

Abu S. (1977), made a study on material beliefs and management strategies of peer interactions as correlates of social comprised of 185 students of pre school children, ranging in age from 44 to 81 months who resided in Seoul, Korea. The result showed that mothers, who assigned greater importance to social skills of their children, were likely to manage their social activities. In addition, mothers who had more efforts to enhance their children's social skills were more likely to have socially competent children with peers.

McCarthy F. (1997), made a study on women instructors in higher education. The researcher's argument is that although women have made significant gains in education at all levels, that their greater participation is marked by a combination of cultural, socio-economic, and psychological factors which influence the fundamental choices they make. It was found in her research that issue of professional opportunity and social recognition; marriage and family relationships present areas of stress and concern for many female scholars.

2.04 Studies on Peer Relations

Oajuja (1992), made an effort to assess the effectiveness of peer tutoring as an instrument in developing the urban and spatial abilities of the students. The major findings of the study were the following. The peer tutoring is significant entirely on academic achievement of the students in the subjects. The teaching strategy was found to be more useful for low and average achieving and learning disabled students. Peer tutoring was helpful in developing a sense of accomplishment in the peer tutoring; the learners received feedback to their performance and get motivated.

Shukla (1992), conducted a study to find out whether peer interactions influence the development of the social competence of the children. The major findings were the following. Peer interactions did reveal highly of significant effects of social competence. The children liked peers have scored significantly higher jeans in all-important competition, social tolerance. Social leadership and social respectability are the least liked peers.

Robertson (1995), conducted an action research on 12 New Zealand Primary School Principals working in partnership to develop their leadership. Findings indicate that peer assisted leadership development helped principals. First of all, it is to focus on their professional and school development goals. Secondly, it reduced their feelings of isolation. Thirdly, it facilitated reflective thinking that lead to proactive and Tran formative action. Fourthly, it leads to the realization of the wider picture of principal's practice in New Zealand.

Slavin (1999), found out the development of social skills and helping skills students learned to value each other and to concentrate on positive relationship. Throughout the year, as new students came into the classes, they were immediately integrated into the teams. Guided interaction around most reluctant teachers becomes actively engaged in learning. Guided peer relations can work wonders in the lives of young students was the most outstanding finding.

Rigby (1997), Who had conducted survey on more than 25 thousand students observed that in the course of anyone year as many as half of the students attending school experience painful and unjustified aggression from students who are physically, psychologically or numerically more powerful than they are. A substantial proportion of these students about 1 in 7, are bullied weekly of more often. Some of these students are very resilient and appear to be unaffected by the emotionally upset or depressed following repeated incidents of peer victimization.

Castor (1993), developed an educational project the peer leader implemented, and evaluated in a rural high school in Australia. Student Peer leaders, identified by social metric methods, volunteered to attend a six day training camp to learn about health and sexuality, to develop social and infer personal skills, and participate in outdoor education activities. On return to their schools, peer leaders, were monitored unobtrusively together with their identified members of their peer group members one month later semi structured interview were conducted with selected peer readers, members of their peer group, parents and teachers. A follow up interview was conducted eight weeks later. The major findings of the project were the following. It accelerated the process of the growth and maturation of the student leaders with regard to their leadership skills. There was a marked improvement in their social development and peer interaction.

Calivari (2001), conducted a study to find out the link between attachment to home and peer relations, attachment to schools and peer relations. A sample of 176 ninth and tenth graders at risk for academic difficulties participated in the study. Result suggested, peer relations influence teenager's satisfaction with school. Peer relations influence one's self-view. Experiences with peer in the school environment can affect one's success in society.

Giles (2004), conducted a study to find out how celebrities influence the younger generation and is related to their social networks. He studied the relationship between celebrity interests, attachment to parents and peer and emotional autonomy among a sample of 191 adolescent who worship celebrities for entertainment and social reasons had a high attachment to peer. They were group players. They were self-confident. Peer interaction is an important feature of celebrity attachment.

Niebrzydowski, L.(1995), studied the Adolescents Family situation and their self-disclosure in interpersonal relationships. This study explored the links between adolescents family situations and their self-disclosure in peer relationships. Participants were 378 pupils between 16 and 18 years of age and the same number of parents of both sexes. The percent belonged to intellectual families and 20 percent to the working class. The study used Journals self-disclosure questionnaire, Algeria's Friendship scale to assess measures of adolescents and parents degrees of self-disclosure and to determine and differentiate interpersonal relationships, and the Family Relationship Test by Anthony and Been to family situation affects adolescents self-disclosure in their contacts with friends; (2) Parental influence is particularly significant when the disclosure of information of personal and intimate character is concerned; and (3) the main factors determining adolescents self disclosure in their contacts with friends are the atmosphere of mutual friendliness and frank and direct communication among family members.

Elizabeth C.W. (1994), studied the Enhance social skills with peer – Recommended books. Discusses how teachers can aid young children in developing social skills in and outside the home through reading and discussing books that present characters and social situations with which children can identity. Discusses several such child-recommended book titles from "children's choice" and includes an annotated bibliography of additional titles dealing with relationships with family, friends, and the larger world. (HTH)

Shmuel S. (1993), studied the close relationships and coping Behavior in Adolescence. Examined role of close relationship during adolescence and their contribution to individual coping. Data from series of studies on early adolescents showed that availability of family and peers combined with support of adolescents independence contributed to individual adaptive coping. Contribution of close relationships to coping differed for males and females. (Authors/NB)

Biglow, - B.J. et al. (1992), studied the social rules that children use: close friends, others friends, and "other rids" compared to parents, Teachers, and siblings. Examined 9-13 year cold's relationship with parents; teachers; siblings; close friends; other friends; and other peers. Used a social rules questionnaire to formulate a checklist of social rules themes. Found that themes that had previously been associated with one class of social relationships had much wider application.

Elizabeth C. et al., (1992), studied the how successful Deaf Teenagers Experience and cope with Isolation. This study examined 23 case studies of outstandingly successful deaf high school students. Analysis indicated that most of the students experienced some degree of isolation from peers, family, or both but had developed positive coping strategies.

CONCLUSION

The review of related literature has helped the investigator to formulate the relevant hypotheses and suitable methodology, which are discussed in the next chapter to follow.

❐

8

Design of the Study and the Method of Investigation

This chapter describes in detail, the design of the study, nature and selection of sample, a brief description of the tools of investigation and the criteria for their investigation. It also gives a description of the procedure adopted for the collection of data, scoring and classification, finally the proposed statisticšl treatment of the data for testing the hypotheses that were formulated are explained.

Hypotheses

1. There is better family relation among high school students.
2. There is better peer relation among high school students.
3. There is significant difference between male and female high school students on their Family Relation.
4. There is significant difference between male and female high school students on their Peer Relation.
5. There is significant difference between High School Students from Nuclear and Joint family on their Family Relation.
6. There is significant difference between High School Students from Nuclear and Joint family on their Peer Relation.
7. There is significant difference between rural and urban high school students on their family relations.

8. There is significant difference between rural and urban high school students on their peer relation.
9. There is significant difference between Tamil and English medium high school students on their family relation
10. There is signification difference between Tamil and English medium high school students on their peer relation.
11. There is significant difference among High School Students of different age groups on their Family Relation.
12. There is significant difference among High School Students of different age groups on their Peer Relation.
13. There is significant difference among High School Students from different Type of Management on their Family Relation.
14. There is significant difference among High School Students from different Type of Management on their Peer Relation.
15. There is significant difference among High School Students of different Parental Qualification in their Family Relation.
16. There is significant difference among High School Students of different Parental Qualification in their Peer Relation.
17. There is significant difference among High School Students Family Income on their Family Relation.
18. There is significant difference among High School Students Family Income on their Peer Relation.
19. There is significant relationship between Family Relation and Peer Relation of high school students.

Tools and Techniques

To test the hypotheses framed, the following tools have been used:

1. Index of Family Relation by Walter W. Hudson
2. Index o Peer Relations by Walter W. Hudson.
3. Index of Family Relations

INDEX OF FAMILY RELATIONS

Description

The English poet John Done wrote, "No man is island, every man is a piece of the continent, a part of the main." For many of us, the continent is our family, those people with who we share ourselves each day. The family can be a source of great positive energy, encouraging us to try new things and supporting us when our attempts fall short. But for some, the family situation is a source of stress and frustration, pulling energy away from us rather than feeding our needs. These needs that are not met belong to all the family members, for no one is immune to the effects of a stressful family life. Children may show it through physical complaints or school problems, while mom and dad may show the pressure in marital conflicts or behavior, which remove them from family contact, such as drinking or an endless list of things to do away from home. Both the individual family members and their intertwined relationship rise or fall on the health of the family unit. For more than thirty years, family researchers have been concerned with the evaluation of the family process. As with any other complex process, attempts have been made to specify what it is in family relationships that can cause problems. Some of the other tests are the results of that work such as marital roles and sexual compatibility, but Dr. Walter Hudson saw the need for a global measure of family satisfaction – an index that went directly to the question, “How do you feel about being a member of this family?” In 1977, he developed the Index of Family Relations as part of his series of tests for use in psychological and social work treatment. It has included because of its

TABLE. 8.1: Showing the Nature of Statements in the Index of Family Relations

S. No	Nature of Statements	Item Numbers	Marks				
			Never	Very Rarely	Some times	Often	Always
1.	Positive	1, 4, 5,8, 14,15, 17, 18, 20, 21, 23	5	4	3	2	1
2.	Negative	2, 3, 6, 7, 9, 10, 11, 12, 13, 16, 19, 22, 24, 25	1	2	3	4	5

Administration

The test is administered to those students who had been randomly chosen from the higher secondary school. The following instructions were given :

- Given below are twenty-five statements regarding family relations.
- Five answers are given beside every statement.

    1. Rarely or None of the time
    2. A little of the time
    3. Some of the time
    4. A good part of the time
    5. Most or all of the time.

- Put a tick mark of the answer, which is most suitable in your opinion. Each statement was read clearly and distinctly so as to enable the students to respond to them with ease. The students were found to be cooperative.

Scoring Procedure

The Index of Family Relations contains both positive and negative statements. The positive items are those, which indicate comfortable family relations among the students. They are the following items : 1, 4, 5, 8, 14, 15, 17, 18, 20, 21 and 23. For the positive statements those who marked Rarely or None of the time. will Score one : A little of the time will score two; Some of the time will score three; A good part of the time will score four; and Most or all of the time will score five.

On the other hand the negative statements indicate difficult family relations. The following items are negative : 2, 3, 6, 7, 9, 10, 11, 12, 13, 16, 19, 22, 24 and 25. For these items those who marked Rarely or none of the time will score five; A little of the time will score four; Some of the time will score three; A good part of the time will score two; and Most or all of the time will score one.

To find total score, the total points of positive items and the total points of negative items are added. From this sum, twenty-five points are subtracted. The result is the final score.

Interpreting the Score

Students who score between 30-100 are comfortable with their present family relations. A high score on this test indicate a low level of family satisfaction. Students who score from 0 to 29 often report significant problems in relating to their family relations.

Establishing Reliability

The reliability of a test may be defined as the degree of consistency with which the test measures what it measures. A test score is called reliable, when we have a reason to believe it to be stable and trustworthy.

Reliability Coefficient of Family Relations

To compute the reliability of Index of Family Relations for the sample shown, the Crookback Alpha Reliability Formula Method was used. The reliability was computed and it was found to be 0.83.

Index of Validity of Family Relation

The validity of Index of Family Relations was found out by computing the square root of the reliability co-efficient which worked out to be 0.91.

INDEX OF PEER RELATION

Description

Everyone has a specific group of people who are important to them. They may be people in the neighborhood, co-workers, or a circle of friends. No matter who they are, peer group serves a very important function for each one. The people in a group provide the guidelines for ones behaviour; social contacts which keep life interesting, and reward, which help to feel good about oneself. In fact, many psychological theories of personality development emphasize the role of peer groups in affecting how one develops as social beings, and with social development comes the related development of personal attitudes and emotional strengths.

In his position as a Professor of Social work, Dr. Walter Hudson became interested in evaluating the impact of peer group satisfaction on the emotional functioning of those in the group. As part of the development of a "clinical measurement package" for use in social work, Dr. Hudson designed the Index of Peer Relations. The test presents a series of straightforward statements, which ask about ones feelings toward those people who may be included in ones, own peer group.

TABLE. 8.2: Showing the nature of statements in the Index Peer Relations

S. No	Nature of Statements	Item Numbers	Marks				
			Never	Very Rarely	Some times	Often	Always
1	Positive	1, 4, 7, 8, 11, 12, 15, 16, 17, 18, 21, 22	5	4	3	2	1
2	Negative	2, 3, 5, 6, 9, 10, 13, 14, 19, 20, 23, 24, 25	1	2	3	4	5

Administration

The test is administered to those students who had been randomly chosen from the science and arts streams of Higher Secondary Schools. Following instructions were given:

- Given below are twenty-five statements regarding peer relations.
- Five answers are given beside every statement.
    1. Rarely or None of the time.
    2. A little of the time.
    3. Some of the time.
    4. A good part of the time
    5. Most or all of the time
- Put a tick mark of the answer, which is most suitable in your opinion.
- The test is to complete within twenty minutes.

Each statement was read clearly and distinctly so as to enable the students to respond to them with ease. The students were found to be cooperative.

Scoring Procedure

The Index of Peer Relations contains both positive and negative statements. The positive items are those which indicate comfortable peer relations among the students. They are the following items: 1, 4, 7, 8, 11, 12, 15, 16, 17, 18, 21 and 22. For the positive statements those who marked Rarely or None of the time will score five; A little of the time will score four; come of the time most or all of the time score three; A good part of the time will score two; and will score one.

On the other hand the negative statements indicate difficult peer relations. The following items are negative: 2, 3, 5, 6, 9, 10, 13, 14, 19, 20, 23, 24 and 25. For these items those who marked Rarely or none of the time will score one; A little of the time will score two; come of the time will score three; A good part of the time, will score four; and motor all of the time will score five.

To find the total score, the total points of positive and negative items are considered. From this twenty-five points are subtracted. The result is the final score.

Interpreting the Score

Students who score between 0 and 30 are comfortable with their present peer group. A low score on this test indicate a high level of satisfaction. Students who score from 31 to 100 often report significant problems in relating to their peer group.

Establishing Reliability

The reliability of a test may be defined as the degree of consistency with which the test measures what it measures. A test score is called reliable, when we have a reason to believe it to be stable and trustworthy.

Reliability Coefficient of Peer Relations

To compute the reliability of Index of Peer Relations for the sample shown, the Combat Alpha Reliability Method was used. The reliability was computed and it was found to be 0.84.

Index of Validity of Peer Relations

The validity of Index of Peer Relations was found out by computing the square root of the reliability co-efficient which worked out to be 0.92.

Pilot Study

A pilot study was conducted to determine the suitability of the tools used in the present investigation. A random sample of 30 students was selected for the study to establish the reliability and validity.

Selection of the Sample

A stratified random sampling technique was adopted for the selection of sample. The schools selected for this study is divided into different strata, namely Government, Government Aided and Un-Aided schools. The random sampling technique was adopted to select the sample. 300 students were taken for the study. 100 students were drawn from Government school, 100 from Un-Aided and 100 from Government Aided schools.

Main Study

The validated tools were made use for the main study to collect the necessary data. The study was carried out in a Government School, an Aided School and an Un-Aided School in Tiruvánnamalai District. In this investigation, the main purpose is to study the family and peer relationship among High School Student.

TABLE. 8.3: Showing the composition of the sample selected for the study: Gender, Type of School, Medium of Instruction, Locate, Age and Type of family wise.

Variables	Categories	Number	Percentage
Gender	Boys	184	61.3
	Girls	116	38.7
Age	13 yrs	40	13.3
	14 yrs	95	31.7
	15 yrs	165	55
Type of School	Un-aided	100	33.3
	Aided	100	33.3
	Govt.	100	33.3
Medium of Instruction	Tamil	200	66.7
	English	100	33.3
Locate	Rural	150	50.0
	Urban	150	50.0
Type of Family	Nuclear family	210	70
	Joint family	90	30

Statistical Techniques

Suitable descriptive and inferential statistical techniques were used in the interpretation of the data to draw out a more meaningful picture of results from the collected data. In the present study the following statistical measures were used:

- Mean
- Standard Deviation
- t-test
- F-ratio
- ANOVA
- Correlation

CONCLUSION

This chapter outlines the design of the present study, the procedure followed and the nature of the sample. It describes the hypotheses to be tested, the tools to be used and the methods of administration and scoring. The method of investigation designed was found to be quite appropriate and effective for the study.

❐

9

Analysis of the Data

This chapter presents the results obtained from the analysis of data collected from the three schools in Tiruvannamalai District, on two variables, namely Family Relation and peer relation. The data has been subjected to various descriptive and inferential statistics. Co-efficient of correlation were also computed for the variable.

Analysis of the Data

The data collected was subjected to statistical calculations and the hypotheses formulated have been verified. The statistics used are the following:

1. Descriptive statistics to understand the nature of Family and Peer Relationship
2. 'f' test to find out the significance of difference between the students based on Age. Type of school, fathers' Qualification types of family, Mothers Qualification and Family Income.
3. 't' test to find out the significance of difference between the students based on Type of Family, Medium of Instruction and Location of the School.
4. Correlation to find out the relationship between Family and Peer Relationship.

Hypothesis I

There is good Family relation among high school students

TABLE. 9.1: Showing frequency and percentage of students with respect to the Family Relation

Category	Frequency	Percentage
Satisfaction	1	0.33%
Good	299	99.67%
Total	300	100%

From the above table it is clear that more number of students lies in above average (99.67%) are having good family relation. Hence, the hypothesis is accepted.

Hypothesis II

There is good Peer Relation among high school students.

TABLE. 9.2: Showing frequency and percentage of students with respect to the Peer Relation.

Category	Frequency	Percentage
Satisfaction	1	0.33%
Good	299	99.67%
Total	300	100%

From the above table, it is clear that more number of students lies in above average (99.67%) Hence the Hypothesis is accepted.

Hypothesis III

There is significant difference between Male and Female High School Students on their Family Relation.

TABLE. 9.3: Showing mean scores of Family Relation of High School Students based on Gender.

Variable	Gender	N	Mean	SD	SEM	CR	LS
Family Relation	Male	184	51.13	7.17	.53	1.016	NS
	Female	116	50.32	6.45	.60		

From the above table, CR value is 1.016 which is lesser than the table value 1.96. There is no significant difference between Male and Female High School Students on their Family Relation. Hence, the Hypothesis is rejected.

Hypothesis IV

There is significant difference between Male and Female High School Students on their Peer Relation.

TABLE. 9.4: Showing mean scores of Peer Relation of High School Students based on Gender.

Variable	Gender	N	Mean	SD	SEM	CR	LS
Peer Relation	Male	184	50.24	6.92	.51	0.698	NS
	Female	116	49.63	7.65	.71		

From the above table, CR Value is 0.698, which is lesser than the table value1.96. There is no significant difference between Male and Female High School Students on their Peer Relation. Hence, the hypothesis is rejected.

Hypothesis V

There is significant difference between High School Students from nuclear and Joint Family on their Family Relation.

TABLE. 9.5: Showing mean scores of Family Relation of High School Students based on Type of Family

Variable	Family	N	Mean	SD	SEM	CR	LS
Family Relation	Nuclear	210	50.65	7.08	.49	.672	NS
	Joint	90	51.21	6.47	.68		

From the above table, CR value is .672, which is lesser than the table value 1.96. There is no significant difference between nuclear and Joint Family"High School Students on their Family Relation. Hence the Hypothesis is rejected.

Hypothesis VI

There is significant difference between High School Students from nuclear and Joint Family on their Peer Relation.

TABLE. 9.6: Showing mean scores of Peer Relation of High School Students based on Type of Family

Variable	Family	N	Mean	SD	SEM	CR	LS
Peer Relation	Nuclear	210	49.74	7.52	.52	1.020	NS
	Joint	90	50.61	6.40	.67		

From the above table, CR value is 1.020, which is lesser than the table value 1.96. There is no significant difference between nuclear and Joint Family High School Students on their Peer Relation. Hence the Hypothesis is rejected.

Hypothesis VII

There is significant difference between Rural and Urban High School Students on their Family Relation.

TABLE. 9.7: Showing mean scores of Family Relation of High School students based on location of the school.

Variable	Locate	N	Mean	SD	SEM	CR	LS
Family Relation	Rural	150	50.51	7.77	.63	.778	NS
	Urban	150	51.13	5.91	.48		

From the above table, CR value is .778, which is lesser than the table value 1.96. There is no significant difference between Rural and Urban High School Students on their Family Relation. Hence the Hypothesis is rejected.

Hypothesis VIII

There is significant difference between rural and urban high school students on their Peer Relation.

TABLE. 9.8: Showing mean scores of Peer Relation of High School Students based on location of the school.

Variable	Locate	N	Mean	SD	SEM	CR	LS
Peer Relation	Rural	150	50.27	7.82	.64	.649	NS
	Urban	150	49.73	6.55	.53		

From the above table, CR value is .649, which is lesser than the table value 1.96. There is no significant difference between Rural and Urban High School Students on their Peer Relation. Hence the Hypothesis is rejected.

Hypothesis IX

There is significant difference between Tamil and English medium high school students on their Family Relation.

TABLE. 9.9: Showing mean scores of Family Relation of High School Students based on Type of Medium.

Variable	Medium	N	Mean	SD	SEM	CR	LS
Family Relation	Tamil	200	50.41	6.79	.48	1.444	NS
	English	100	51.64	7.08	.71		

From the above table, CR value is 1.444, which is lesser than the table 1.96. There is no significant difference between Tamil and English medium high school students on their Family Relation. Hence the Hypothesis is rejected.

Hypothesis X

There is significant difference between Tamil and English medium high school students on their Peer Relation.

TABLE. 9.10: Showing mean scores of Peer Relation of High School Students based on Type of Medium.

Variable	Medium	N	Mean	SD	SEM	CR	LS
Peer Relation	Tamil	200	49.71	6.89	.49	957	NS
	English	100	50.59	7.80	.78		

From the above table, CR value is .957, which is lesser than the table Value 1.96. There is no significant difference between Tamil and English medium high school students on their Peer Relation. Hence the Hypothesis is rejected.

Hypothesis XI

There is significant difference among high school students of different age group on their Family Relation.

TABLE. 9.11: Showing the mean scores of Family Relation among different Age Group of High School Students

Variable	Group	Sum of Squares	Df	Mean Squares	F-value	LS
Family Relation	Between group	76.457	2	38.228	.802	NS
	Within group	14154.460	297	47.658		
	Total	14230.917	299			

From the above table F-value .802, which is lesser than the table value1.96. There is no significant difference among high school students of different age groups on their Family Relation. Hence the hypothesis is rejected

Hypothesis XII

There is significant difference among high school students of different age group on their Peer Relation.

TABLE. 9.12: Showing the mean scores of Peer Relation among different Age Group of High School Students

Variable	Group	Sum of Squares	Df	Mean Squares	F-value	LS
Peer Relation	Between group	125.956	2	62.978	1.215	NS
	Within group	15391.041	297	51.822		
	Total	15516.997	299			

From the above table F-value 1.215, which is lesser than the table value1.96. There is no significant difference among high school students of different age groups on their Peer Relation. Hence the hypothesis is rejected

Hypothesis XIII

There is significant difference among high school students of different types of management on their Family Relation.

TABLE. 9.13: Showing the mean scores of Family Relation among different Type of Management of High School Students

Variable	Group	Sum of Squares	Df	Mean Squares	F-value	LS
Family Relation	Between group	103.487	2	51.743	1.088	NS
	Within group	14127.430	297	47.567		
	Total	14230.917	299			

From the above table F-value 1.088, which is lesser than the table value 1.96. There is no significant difference among high school students of different types of management on their Family Relation. Hence the hypothesis is rejected.

Hypothesis XIV

There is significant difference among high school students of different types of management on their Peer Relation.

TABLE. 9.14: Showing the mean scores of peer relation among different type of Management High School Students

Variable	Group	Sum of Squares	Df	Mean Squares	F-value	LS
Peer Relation	Between group	51.627	2	25.813	.496	NS
	Within group	15465.370	297	52.072		
	Total	15516.997	299			

From the above table F-value .496, which is lesser than the table, value 1.96.There is no significant difference among high school students of different types of management on their Peer Relation. Hence the hypothesis is rejected

Hypothesis XV

There is significant difference among high school students of different father qualification in their Family Relation.

TABLE. 9.15: Showing the Mean scores of Family Relation among different type of Father Qualification High School Students

Variable	Group	Sum of Squares	Df	Mean Squares	F-value	LS
Family Relation	Between group	62.704	2	31.352	.657	NS
	Within group	14168.212	297	47.704		
	Total	**14230.917**	**299**			

From the above table F-value .657, which is lesser than the table, value 1.96.There is no significant difference among high school students of different father qualification in their Family Relation. Hence the hypothesis is rejected.

Hypothesis XVI

There is significant difference among high school students of different types of management on their Peer Relation.

TABLE. 9.16: Showing the mean scores of Peer Relation among different type of Father Qualification High School Students

Variable	Group	Sum of Squares	Df	Mean Squares	F-value	LS
Peer Relation	Between group	13.688	2	6.844	.131	NS
	Within group	15503.309	297	52.200		
	Total	**15516.997**	**299**			

From the above table F-value .131, which is lesser than the table value 1.96. There is no significant difference among high school students of different father qualification inn their Peer Relation. Hence the hypothesis is rejected.

Hypothesis XVII

There is significant difference among high school students of different Mother Qualification in their Family Relation.

TABLE 9.17: Showing the mean scores of Family Relation among different type of Mother Qualification High School Students

Variable	Group	Sum of Squares	Df	Mean Squares	F-value	LS
Family Relation	Between group	45.937	2	22.969	.481	NS
	Within group	14184.980	297	47.761		
	Total	**14230.917**	**299**			

From the above table F-value .481, which is lesser than the table value 1.96. There is no significant difference among high school students of different Mother Qualification in their Family Relation. Hence the hypothesis is rejected.

Hypothesis XVIII

There is significant difference among high school students of different Mother Qualification in their Peer Relation.

TABLE. 9.18: Showing the Mean scores of Peer Relation among different type of Mother Qualification High School Students

Variable	Group	Sum of Squares	Df	Mean Squares	F-value	LS
Peer Relation	Between group	42.267	2	21.133	.406	NS
	Within group	15474.730	297	52.103		
	Total	15516.997	299			

From the above table F-value .406, which is lesser than the table, value 1.96.Tthere is no significant difference among high school students of different Mother Qualification in their Peer Relation. Hence the hypothesis is rejected.

Hypothesis XIX

There is significant difference among high school students of different Parent Annual Income on their Family Relation.

TABLE. 9.19: Showing the Mean Scores of Family Relation among different type of Parent Annual Income High School Students

Variable	Group	Sum of Squares	Df	Mean Squares	F-value	LS
Family Relation	Between group	70.593	2	35.296	.740	NS
	Within group	14160.324	297	47.678		
	Total	14230.917	299			

From the above table F-value .740, which is lesser than the table value 1.96. There is no significant difference among high school students of different Parent Annual Income on their Family Relation. Hence the hypothesis is rejected

Hypothesis XX

There is significant difference among high school students of different Parent Annual Income on their Peer Relation.

TABLE. 9.20: Showing the Mean Scores of Peer Relation among different type of Parents Annual Income High School Students

Variable	Group	Sum of Squares	Df	Mean Squares	F-value	LS
Family Relation	Between group	81.517	2	40.758	.784	NS
	Within group	15435.480	297	51.971		
	Total	15516.997	299			

From the above table F-value .784, which is lesser than the table value 1.96.There is no significant difference among high school students of different Parent Annual Income on their Peer Relation. Hence the hypothesis is rejected.

Hypothesis XXI

There is significant relationship between family relation and peer relation of high School students Correlation Co-efficient and level of significance for the variables Family Relations and Peer relationship.

TABLE. 9.21: Showing the Correlation between Family Relations and Peer Relationship among High School Students

Correlation Co-efficient

Variable	Correlation Co-efficient	LS
Family Relationship Vs Peer Relationship	0.1726	0.05

From the above table it is observed there is relationship between Family Relation and Peer Relation among the High School Students and so the hypothesis is retained.

CONCLUSION

A brief report of the research study together with major findings and conclusion arrived at, along with their educational implications have been presented in the succeeding chapter. ❐

10

Summary, Findings and Conclusion

A brief summary of the study, stating the problem, the objective, the methodology and the major findings are presented in this chapter. The implications of the study are then discussed, suggesting a few areas for further research.

Statement of the Problem

A study of Family and Peer Relationship among the High School Students.

KEYWORDS IN THE STATEMENT

Family Relationship

Family Relationship in the present study is a measure of the individual's reaction towards his family members. Family Relationship as measured through this inventory is an assessment of factors such as sense of personal feelings with his father, mother and other family members.

Peer Group Relationship

The way in which the High School Students relate to one another, interact with one another and communicate with one another indicate their level of Peer Relation.

Objectives of the Study

1. To find out the level of Family Relation among High School Students.
2. To find out the level of Peer Relation among High School Students.
3. To find out the significant difference between male and female High Students on their Family Relation.
4. To find out the significant difference between male and female High School Students on their Peer Relation.
5. To find out the significant difference between high school student from nuclear and Joint family on their Family Relation
6. To find out the significant difference between high school student from nuclear and Joint family on their Peer Relation.
7. To find out the significant difference between rural and urban high school students on their family relations.
8. To find out the significant difference between rural and urban high school students on their peer relation.
9. To find out the significant difference between Tamil and English medium high school students on their family relation.
10. To find out the significant different between Tamil and English medium high school students on their peer relation.
11. To find out the significant difference among High School students of different age groups on their family relation
12. To find out the significance difference among High School Students of different age groups on their peer relation
13. To find out the significant difference among High School Students of different type of management on their Family Relation.
14. To find out the significant difference among High School Students from different Type of management on their Peer Relation.
15. To find out the significant different among High School Students of different Parental Qualification in their Family Relation.
16. To find out the significant difference among High School Students of different Parental Qualification in their Peer Relation.
17. To find out the significant difference among high school students of different family income on their Family Relation.
18. To find out the significant difference among high school students of different family income on their Peer Relation.
19. To find out the significant relationship between Family Relation and Peer Relation of high school student.

Hypotheses

1. There is better Family Relation among High School Students
2. There is better Peer Relation among High School Students
3. There is significant difference between male and female high school students on their Family Relation.
4. There is significant difference between male and female high school students on their Peer Relation.
5. There is significant difference between High School Students from Nuclear and Joint family on their Family Relation.
6. There is significant difference between High School Students from Nuclear and Joint family on their Peer Relation.
7. There is significant difference between rural and urban high school students on their family relations.
8. There is significant difference between rural and urban high school students on their peer relation.
9. There is significant difference between Tamil and English medium high school students on their family relation
10. There is signification difference between Tamil and English medium high school students on their peer relation.
11. There is significant difference among High School Students of different age groups on their Family Relation.
12. There is significant difference among High School Students of different age groups on their Peer Relation.
13. There is significant difference among High School Students from different Type of Management on their Family Relation.
14. There is significant difference among High School Students from different Type of Management on their Peer Relation.
15. There is significant difference among High School Students of different Parental Qualification in their Family Relation.
16. There is significant difference among High School Students of different Parental Qualification in their Peer Relation.
17. There is significant difference among High School Students Family Income on their Family Relation.
18. There is significant difference among High School Students Family Income on their Peer Relation.
19. There is significant relationship between Family Relation and Peer Relation of high school students.

Major Findings

1. It is found that there is good Family Relation among high school students.
2. It is found that there is good peer relation among High School students
3. It is found that there is no significant different between male and female high school students of their family relation
4. It is found that there is no significant different between male and female high school students of their peer relation
5. It is found that there is no significant different between nuclear and joint family high school students on their family relation
6. It is found that there is no significant different between nuclear and joint family high school students on their peer relation.
7. It is found that there is no significant different between rural and urban high school students on their family relation
8. It is found that there is no significant different between rural and urban high school students on their peer relation.
9. It is found that there is significant difference between Tamil and English medium high school students on their family relation.
10. It is found that there is no significant difference between Tamil and English medium high school students on their peer relation.
11. It is found that there is no significant difference among high school students of different age groups on their family relation.
12. It is found that there is no significant difference among high school students of difference age groups on their peer relation.
13. It is found that there is no significant difference among high school students of different type of management on their family relation.
14. It is found that there is no significant difference among high school students of different types of management on their peer relation
15. It is found that there is no significant difference among high school students of different father qualification on their family relation
16. It is found that there is no significant difference among high school students of different father qualification on their peer relation
17. It is found that there is no significant difference among high school students of different mother qualification on their family relation.
18. It is found that there is no significant different among high school students of different mother qualification on their peer relation.
19. It is found that there is no significant difference among high school students of different parent annual income on their family relation.
20. It is found that there is no significant difference among high school students of different parent annual income on their peer relation.

21. It is found that correlation there is significant relationship between family relation and peer relation of high school students.

Sample

The sample population consisted of 300 IX and X standard students. The samples were taken from three schools in Tiruvannamalai District. There were 100 samples from each school. The three schools are one Government school, one Aided school and Private School.

Tools and Techniques

To test the hypotheses framed, the following tool has been used:

- Index of Family Relations by Walter W. Hudson.
- Index of Peer Relation by Walter W.Hudson.

Educational Implications

Very frequently schools criticize parents for sending children to them who are untrained and parents in turn criticize schools for not doing a good job. Negative blaming is not useful in raising children. Cooperation between the home and the school can greatly benefit all concerned. When a partnership exits between teachers and parents and if they use similar successful methods then children prepare for life and their academic achievement will be meritorious. Hence, the most important educational implication is that of cooperation and mutual support and encouragement between teachers and parents.

Limitations of the Study

- The sample is restricted to 300 students.
- The study is restricted IX and X standard students.
- The study is limited to 3 types of schools in Tirunvannamalai District. Via Government School, an Aided School, and Private

Suggestions for further Research

1. The present study is confined only to students of higher secondary level in Thiruvannamalai educational district. To make the findings of this study more universal a cross cultural study may be conducted.
2. This study may be conducted among college students.
3. Psychological variable like achievement motivation, level of aspiration may be incorporated in this study.

CONCLUSION

The purpose of the present investigation was to family relation and peer relationship. The study is sore to find some usefulness in the field of Education and Findings of the study conserve as a database for further research. ❐

11

The Problem and its Perspectives

The importance of teaching thinking skills, including the ability to identify novel and effective solutions to unstructured problems, has long been considered an important goal for educators. It is particularly important for teacher educators who are seeking to prepare students. In the psychology literature a substantial body of research has been developed that specifically addresses the factors that can be managed to facilitate and motivate the creative process. The components, creativity relevant skills, domain relevant sills, and motivation, are identified as necessary and sufficient for creativity in any domain. The development of domain relevant skills, such as domain relevant knowledge and specific analytic tools, are identified as being important and within the ambit of the teacher trainees.

THE CONCEPT OF CREATIVITY

The term creativity is widely used with reference to the creative people, the creative process, even a creative environment (Brown 1989). Our interest is in the process, culminating in a novel and effective solution to an open-ended problem. The importance of both novelty and effectiveness is reflected in the following definition. Creativity is the ability to produce work that is both novel and appropriate (Sternberg 1988). This definition is widely accepted in the creativity literature (Amabile 1966; Sternberg 1999). However, environmental factors will interact with individual differences and influence the creative process (Amabile 1996). Focusing on the process, and the facts that will influence that process, highlighting the implications for addressing heuristic (open-ended) problems within a teaching course in ways that support the creative process. Guilford (1950) made an important contribution to our understanding of creativity when he distinguished between convergent and divergent thinking processes. Convergent thinking is similar to conventional notions of intelligence in which existing knowledge / information is synthesized to arrive at the single most appropriate answer. Guilford argued that creativity is expressed in terms of divergent thinking, however this led to measuring creativity in terms of the number of fundamentally different solutions that were generated (e.g., Torrance 1974). This emphasis on divergent thinking and novelty is consistent with the typical layperson's conception of creativity.

Many of the theorists who have modeled the creative process incorporate both divergent and convergent thinking processes. There is a role for divergent thinking in order to recognize previously unnoticed problems and in exploring possible responses. However, convergent thinking is also important as relevant information is identified and brought to bear on the problem. The recognition that both divergent and convergent thinking is important in the creative process is important for educators because the way in which problems are presented and evaluated will have an impact on a student's thinking process. The following sections describe the creative process and consider the implications for facilitating and motivating Guilford (1950) made an important contribution to our understanding of creativity when he distinguished between convergent and divergent thinking processes. Convergent thinking is similar to conventional notions of intelligence in which existing knowledge / information is synthesized to arrive at the single most appropriate answer. Guilford argued that creativity is expressed in terms of divergent thinking, however this led to measuring creativity in terms of the number of fundamentally different solutions that were generated that process in the classroom.

THE CREATIVE PROCESS

Creativity was initially studied as an intellectual or personality trait. The emphasis was on the creative individual and the nature of creativity was considered to be a black box' (Barron and Harrington 1981). More recently, however, there have been various attempts to describe and model the creative process so that it can then be effectively managed.

Amabile (1996) describes four phases in the creative process, namely: 1. Problem identification, 2. Preparation, 3. Response generation, and 4.Validation and communication. Other theorists describe similar phases, for example, preparation, incubation, illumination, and verification (Wallas 1926) on preparation, Production, evaluation, and implementation (Hogarth 1980). In this section Amabil's model of the creative process is presented to provide a context for the subsequent discussion of motivating and facilitating creativity in the classroom. Amabil's model was chosen because she has devoted particular attention to the positive effect that expected evaluation and rewards can have when applied appropriately to the various phases of the creative process. The first step in the creative process is to identify that a problem exists (Runco and Chand 1994). The problem may be presented to the individual, or recognition that a problem exists may be generated internally. Getzels and Csikszentmihallyi (1976) suggest that 'discovered problems' are more likely to be solved creatively than 'presented problems'. Furthermore, always presenting the student with a predetermined problem ignores the importance of problem identification skills.

Problem based learning emphasizes the importance of student's identifying the problem for themselves whereas case studies tend to be more focused and direct the student to address specific issues / problems. The importance of identifying and responding to the root cause of a problem rather than symptoms may be the most important determinant of successful innovation in schools.

As noted by Thomas (1999) problem symptoms are often mistakenly identified as problems, resulting in waste efforts at solving something that was not a problem. Through appropriate instruction students can develop the skills necessary to think beyond sterepriate instruction students can develop the skills necessary to think beyond stereotypical conceptions of the problem. When a problem has been identified, preparation includes building up or reactivating relevant information. The way in which an individual combines and reorganizes information in the preparation phase plays a crucial role in the generation of responses. Finke, Ward and Smith (1992) note that the combination and reorganization efforts can bring new features to the forefront that may lead to a reconceptualisation of the initial problem. Therefore, the problem may be redefined, leading to a very different solution, depending on the way in which the information is analyzed.

Amabile (1996) notes that this is one of the 'perspiration' phases of the creative process that individuals may seek to bypass, moving too quickly to the more intrinsically motivating idea generation phase. The response generation phase determines the extent to which the solution will be novel. Moving too quickly through this phase may limit the number of possible responses since obvious ideas is usually generated first, and, only when these are exhausted, more remote association are found (Runco and Sakamoto 1999). Here the ability to suspend critical judgment is important. Brainstorming (Osborn 1953) is one technique that has been proposed to increase the number of responses. It involves creating a non-threatening atmosphere to avoid inhibitions. The final solution will be chosen from the ideas that have been generated. While there is some support (Milgram and Rabkin 1978) for a positive relationship between the quantity and quality of responses, the quality of responses generated will also be determined by the level of understanding of the problem space.

FACTORS INFLUENCING THE CRATIVE PROCESS

Amabile (1983) argues that creativity is best conceptualized not as a personality Trait or as a general ability, but as a behavior resulting from particular constellations of personal characteristics, cognitive abilities, and social environments. This view was shared by most contemporary theorists (Mumford et.al 1993) who emphasize changing the environment in order to promote and facilitate creativity. It is particularly relevant for educators wishing to establish an environment that supports creativity by managing the factors that promote or inhibit it. Amabil's componential model of creativity specifically recognizes the importance of domain-relevant skills, motivation and creativity relevant skills.

EDUCATION AND SOCIETY

Education is the fulcrum upon which hangs the peaceful evolutionary transition of Society. It plays a vital role in building a society. A modern society cannot achieve its aim of economic growth, technical development and cultural advancement without fully harnessing the talents of its citizens. For the advancement in education proper social maturity, values and adjustment pattern should be there. Social maturity, values and adjustment pattern should be there. Social maturity is related to values that are found in the society. Teacher educators are very well associated with the cultivation of social maturity among the student teachers. Then only they will develop an integrated personality, proper cultivation of values to cope with the environment amicably.

Man doesn't stand-alone; he is only and essentially a social animal, otherwise he may describe as a "beast" or a "god" but not as a "man". Similarly society is just an abstraction unless it mirrors the human values, norms, ambitions and goals society is never an aggregate of individuals. It's, in the sense, no predictable string of unity. Tandra Patanic (1986) states, "The society is rather a peculiar amalgamation of unity and diversity, which characterizes the society that again reflects the nature of human mind" (p.40). Mind can be judged from various sensitivity and emotionality. Separately none of these qualities of the mind can be called to constitute the proper essence of the mind. So man and the society and their relation have been viewed here as a prism throwing multi-colored spectrum of light. Yet the arrangement of colour may change in the direction of the light. Society is a prism; it has multiple facets along with its unique ability of adapting to the changes of circumstances.

EDUCATION AS AN AGENCY OF SOCIETY

The process of education is of deep significance to the growth and welfare of society. If the people are to keep pace with the fast changing social order, with scientific discoveries and with the explosion of knowledge in all parts of the world, the hidden talents of youth must be brought to the surface and be exploited for the good of the society. There is a great demand for creative ideas and creative talents, and education is the best means for the developments of such talents. The events of our time are moving continually, accelerating the rate and if the people are to keep pace with them, the people must make sure that the talents of the youth are thoroughly developed.

Alexander. A. Schaeiders (1965) defines "Education is the total experiences that can transform the life of the individual person". Education can contribute much and in many different ways to the social, moral and religious growth of the adolescent to healthy social perspectives to adequate vocational attitudes and goals, and to the future roles that the adolescent will expect to play. By means of active participation on the playing field and through extracurricular activities such as oratory, debating, newspaper reporting or yearbook editing the adolescent can pick up many ideas, skills and general know-how that may be of great help to him later in his social relations and vocational aspirations.

MATURITY AS A DETERMINANT OF PERSONALITY

Henery. E. Garett (2968) says, "Social maturity is the degree of social participation as Measured by child's activities, attitudes and play interests. It is related to physical growth and maturity and to mental ability".

One of the components of social maturity is adjustment. Maturity is the determinant of personality. A man's personality is the total picture of his organized behavior, especially as it can be characterized by his fellow men in a consistent way.

An individual, since his birth attempts to interest with his environment. Behavior of an individual can be defined as an adjustment to his environment. Every individual develops his own unique way of adjustment in the society. Socially matured individuals are better able to adjust to the various changes in the environment and react appropriately, thus making the right type of adjustment.

IMPORTANCE OF MATURITY

Nazarth Maria E. Waples (1978) defines, "Maturity is the blossoming of man's Character into a unified totality. It discerns the processes that contribute to the psychological and physical growth and well-being of man".

Maturity assumes accountability, constantly assesses, judges and taken appropriate decisions. Maturity develops a balanced emotional outlook, helping the individual to accept himself, his talents and limitation and to accept others as they are. It analyses values and internalized them consistently. It helps towards progressive advancement in spiritual growth, impelling the individual to adapt himself to change and to life without emotional crises. Abraham Sperling (1967) states social maturity in the following words "An adolescent should get along with and well with others. He ought to develop self-reliance in matters of taste and ought to develop tolerance of human differences." Maturity is gradual process that comes with self-knowledge and with self-realization shaping man into a responsible adult.

CHARACTERISTICS OF SOCIALLY MATURED INDIVIDUAL

Social maturity is evidenced in the capacity of the individual to maintain Friendships that meet the needs of others as well as his own. Vatsysyan (1990) states "A mature individual from the social stand point is one who co-operates with all those with whom be comes into contact and contradicts them only when such a course of actions becomes inevitable. He is never ill-mannered choosing instead to appear very well mannered, considerate and friendly to all and sundry" (P.119), consequently has a large circle of friends. An adult, who has attended that stage as required by the standpoint, evinces great interest in art, study, games etc.

He studies the works of greatest authors and taken interest in games and forms of recreation suitable to his station in life. His activities and conduct are scrupulously in conformity with his age and sex. He has the power of independent decision and judgment. He gives every evidence of being well balanced and adjusted with himself and his behavior towards other individuals.

Elizabeth B.Hurlock (1959) says, "The socially mature individual has a sense of his proper place and role as a member of a group. He is willing and able to orient himself in the various activities with others and customs of the group, to make the proportionate contribution to the work to be done, to take a suitable part in the social exchange to assume a reasonable amount of responsibility and to adjust himself to the inevitable limitations and restrictions of community life without waste of energy or loss of satisfaction." He can be original and yet conform to the broad pattern of the cultural environment.

Taneja R.P. (1989) says, "Social maturity refers to degree of growth in social and vocational abilities." The Socially mature individual treats the members of his family as friends. In this role he shows the affection, loyalty, consideration and respect for all family members. As a citizen the socially mature person accepts his obligations and performs them faithfully. He makes good adjustments to all types of people without prejudice based on their religion, race or skin colour.

The matured accepts his friends as they are and does not criticize or try to change them as a socially immature person does. He is loyal to them and feels a sense of responsibility towards them when they need his help. Although social life may add greatly to his happiness, the mature person is self-sufficient enough that he can be happy when circumstances make it possible for him to be with his family, friends or acquaintances.

The mature individual can be found to possess the trait of good humour and pleasantness. The important point is that he keeps himself alive, with vigorous interests that make him interesting to be with. The mature individual possess a feeling of social concern and gets very involved in situations that call for obedience to social norms too. The person equipped with the human sensitivities that make for maturity will usually have powerful concern with social problems and ways of alleviating them. For all his savoring of human relationships, the maturing individual is not dependent on always having company.

The mature person knows that he has to go on choosing alternatives, that each alternative costs him something, and there are things he will never be able to do and experience. He also knows that there are things he will never be able to do again, that he can never recapture his youth or relive his first encounters with certain experiences. He knows that his integrity is continually threatened by practical demands, by seductive temptations, by concessions and compromises, by conflicting values, and can only real rewards in life come with continued growth, and that there is no room in the one material life he has for major regrets. This individual who has approached maturity can know that he has loved, had loved, had done his work, and has made his mark on people.

STATEMENT OF THE PROBLEM

The Problem is titled ***"Creativity and Social Maturity of Teacher Trainees."***

SIGNIFICANCE OF THE STUDY

Social maturity can only be found through self-knowledge and self - control, based on the objective existence of a science of human nature. In order to protect socially supported beliefs and conventions, society employs a complex system of prohibitions, backed up by ostracism and punishment.

Society sets up a system of socially convenient belief for truth, and conventional patterns of behavior for what are right. The individual who chooses to live outside this system has two fold tasks, to make his peace with society at adaptive level, and to maintain always his own independent standards of what a high quality life is all about. To accomplish this end he must be able to see what is compulsive or obsessive in himself, working to reduce or eliminate these influences in his life without losing track of the wisdom and strength he already has. His motivation for doing this is the promotion of his own mental health there is no ostracism, only selective withdrawal, and no punishment, only selective indifference. Identity is carried by their devotion to the quality of living for themselves and others, and is not invested in career success, ethnic identity, or in their ability to survive through coping with recurrent psychological crises.

Social maturity is the final expected outcome of social development. The socially matured person knows his role as a member of the social group. The person will organize himself socially and will take part in various activities and customs of the group. A person with high social maturity will know the responsibilities and will be able to adjust himself in the society as he would have good creativity so as to solve the problems of the students. So it is significant to study the social maturity and creativity of the secondary grade teacher trainees, as it is essential for the classroom teaching and effective interaction.

OBJECTIVES OF THE STUDY

1. To find out the significance of difference in the fluency level of men and women teacher trainees.
2. To find out the significance of difference in the flexibility level of men and women teacher trainees.
3. To find out the significance of difference in the originality level of men of women teacher trainees.
4. To find out the significance of difference in the personal adequacy of men and women teacher trainees.
5. To fine out the significance of difference in the interpersonal adequacy of men and women teacher trainees.
6. To find out the significance of difference in the social adequacy of men and women teacher trainees.
7. To find out of the significance of difference in the social maturity of men and women teacher trainees.
8. To find out the significance of difference between teacher trainees studying in Government and Government aided institutions with respect to fluency level.
9. To find out the significance of difference between teacher trainees studying in Government and Government aided institutions with respect to flexibility level.

10. To find out the significance of difference between teacher trainees studying in Government and Government aided institutions with respect to originality level.
11. To find out the significance to difference between teacher trainees studying in Government and Government Aided institutions with respect to personal adequacy in social maturity.
12. To find out the significance of difference between teacher trainees studying in Government and Government Aided institutions with respect to Interpersonal adequacy in social maturity.
13. To find out the significance of difference between teacher trainees studying in Government and Government Aided institutions with respect to social adequacy in social maturity.
14. To find out the significance of difference between teacher trainees studying in Government and Government Aided institutions with respect to overall social maturity.
15. To find out the significance of difference between teachers trainees studying in first year and second year with respect to fluency level in creativity.
16. To find out the significance of difference between teachers trainees studying in first year and second year with respect to flexibility level in creativity.
17. To find out the significance of difference between teachers trainees studying in first year and second year with respect to originality level in creativity.
18. To find out the significance of difference between teachers trainees studying in first year and second year with respect to personal adequacy in the social maturity scale.
19. To find out the significance of difference between teachers trainees studying in first year and second year with respect to interpersonal adequacy in the social maturity scale.
20. To find out the significance of difference between teachers trainees studying in first year and second year with respect to social adequacy in the social maturity scale.
21. To find out the significance of difference between teachers trainees studying in first year and second year with respect to overall social maturity.
22. To find out the significance of difference between the teacher trainees in the creativity factors based on their father's qualifications.
23. To find out the significance of difference between the teacher trainees in the social maturity based on their father's qualifications.

24. To find out the significance of difference between the teacher trainees in the creativity factors based on their mother's qualifications.
25. To find out the significance of difference between the teacher trainees in the social maturity based on their mother's qualifications.
26. To find out the significance of difference between the teacher trainees in the creativity factors based on their parental income.
27. There is significant relationship between creativity dimensions and personal adequacy of teacher trainees.
28. There is significant relationship between creativity dimensions and interpersonal adequacy of teacher trainees.
29. There is significant relationship between creativity dimensions and social adequacy of teacher trainees.
30. There is significant relationship between creativity dimensions and social maturity of teacher trainees.
31. There is significant relationship between creativity dimensions and social maturity of teacher trainees.

CONCLUSION

The first chapter is chiefly concerned with the conceptual frame work of the problem. The discussion on creativity and has been presented to highlight the conceptual position with which this study has been placed and conducted. Having acquainted with the necessary theoretical aspects of social maturity and creativity the investigator has reviewed the related research conducted by the educational experts in India and abroad. The summary of related literature is presented in the next chapter.

❒

12

Review of Related Literature

An essential part of research project is the review of studies related to the present investigation. The terms 'Review' means revision or glances over, or refers back on. Review of research studies pertaining to the problem under investigation is of fundamental importance. The present chapter summarizes research studies related to the problem "Creativity and Social Maturity of Teacher Trainees."

STUDIES ON CREATIVITY

INDIAN STUDIES

Dubey Sushma (1986) investigated into the Educational influences on development of Creative thinking in children. It was assumed that there is a symbolize relationship between natural / social environment and creative thinking. The hypotheses of the study were; there will be positive association between age and creative thinking there will be positive association between enriched school education environment and creative thinking and there will be positive association between enriched family environment and creative thinking.

The sample consisted of 255 male students (130 from an enriched school education environment and 125 from an impoverished school education environment) The tools administered were kuppuswamy's Scocio Economic status scale, Baquer Mehdi's Non verbal Test of Creative Thinking and Passi's Puzzle test. The data obtained were subjected to multifactor analysis of variance, correlation analysis and factor analysis. The major findings were

Age, School, Education environment; family education environment and socio class were found to have significant positive main effects on creative thinking in children. The interaction between age and space, space and school education environment, and school education environment and family education environment had significant effect on creative thinking.

Golwalkar (1986) in his study on the scientific attitude, creativity and achievement used a sample of 270 tribal non-tribal students of Rajestan studying in classes IX and X offering science as an optional subject.

The main objectives of the research were to study the scientific attitude of tribal and non-tribal students, to compare the creativity of tribal and non-tribal students and to compare the achievement of tribal and non-tribal students in science subjects.

The tools were Scientific Attitude Scale, Thinking Creativity with words and Thinking Creativity with figures. Analysis of data revealed that: non-tribals were found to be superior to tribals on three components of scientific attitude, the non-tribals had a higher level of creativity than the tribals and the non-tribal students had a higher level of scholarly achievement in science subjects than the tribal students.

Desai (1987) investigated into the creative thinking ability of students of higher secondary of Gujarat state in the context of some psycho-socio factors. The objective was to study the creative thinking ability in relation to scholastic achievement, anxiety and reasoning ability. The sample consisted of 608 students. Analysis of data revealed that: there was no difference in creative thinking ability of urban and rural higher secondary students, the students with higher scholastic achievement were found better in creative thinking than students with scholastic achievement and the students with good reasoning ability were better in creative thinking than students with poor reasoning ability.

Raina (1986) investigated into psychosocial correlates of scientific creativity among high school students. The aims of the study were to find out the relationship between scientific creativity and achievement in science for boys and girls, to study the effect of sex and type of school on scientific creativity among high school students, to study the effect of socio economic status, sex problem solving ability and achievement in science on scientific creativity and to study the effect of sex, birth order and type of family on scientific creativity.

The tools administered on a sample of 1000 students (459 boys and 541 girls) were the Gupta Scientific Creativity Test, Achievement Test in Science and the Socio Economic Status scale.

The noted findings were Achievement in science was significantly related with scientific creativity, the mean scientific creativity score of high achievers in science was more than that of middle and low achievers. Middle achievers were more creative than low achievers in science, first - born students were more creative in science than second and third borne and students belonging to middle socio economic status and having high achievement scores were highest in scientific creativity.

Trimurthy (1987) investigated into the Creative Thinking Ability of Secondary school students in the context of some Psych-socio Factors. The objectives of the study were to study the trends of creative thinking ability in relation to age and to study the relationship of socio economic status with creative thinking ability.

The sample consisted of 603 secondary school students. Results indicated that: boys were better than the girls in both verbal and non-verbal creative thinking ability and urban students were better than the rural students in both verbal and non-verbal creative thinking ability students with high IQ were found to be more creative than students with low IQ in verbal creative thinking ability.

FOREIGN STUDIES

The effect of intelligence, creativity, and cognitive style on success in composition was studied by Meduffie, Harriet E. (1988). This is a descriptive study of 109 college freshmen at a small southern public university which used the Torrance Tests of Creative Thinking Verbal (TTCT), the Otis-Lennon School Abilities Test (OLSAT), and the Cognitive Style Map (CSM), and an average score of two Writing Samples to obtain a composite portrait of a successful academic writer. The findings of the study demonstrate that students with high performance scores in writing are more affected by intelligence and cognitive style than by creativity. In fact, creativity scores on originality had no co relational significance with success in academic writing performance.

Keith James (1991) investigated Personality, Cognitive Skills, and Creativity in Different Life Domains. A preliminary effort was made to integrate personality and cognitive-skill approaches to understanding the sources of creativity. It was proposed that personality and cognitive skill each have differential predicative power for different types (i.e., domains) of creativity. Further, it was proposed that cognitive skills at least partially mediate personality effects on creativity and that personality and cognitive skills may interact to shape creativity. Both personality and divergent thinking measures were used to predict 3 types of creativity-problem solving, artistic, and social-among 41 students in a creativity course. Results of vicariate correlation, analysis of variance, and regression analyses provided some support for the ideas that (a) different types of creativity are somewhat independent of each other, (b) personality and divergent thinking have somewhat different relations to creativity of different types, (c)originality of thinking partially medicates the relations of personality to creativity in different domains, and (d) personality and divergent thinking have some interactive, as well as some main effect, impacts on creativity.

Weinerman, Ilene (1997) conducted a study on creativity in the classroom; an examination of student teacher personality and perceptions of the classroom setting (preservice). The Purpose of this study was to identify the positive and negative relationship between creativity and personality, as well as the direction and degree of association among creativity, personality, and the student teacher's classroom emphasis and orientation. An additional purpose was the development and testing of a path model to determine whether causal linkages can be established among these same sets of variables. Specifically examined were the direct effects of personality and creativity, as well as the significance of creativity as an intervening variable with indirect effect on perceptions of the classroom setting.

Singh (1986) assessed achievement motivation, level of aspiration, and anxiety as correlates of creativity among denotified tribal (DT) children. The author compared 450 denotified tribe children and 450 students from ashram-type and general schools. In view of the lower level of functioning of DT children the author suggested formal education from the nursery stage for them; more of vocational and physical facilities, scope for inter-personal relationships, and psycho-educational guidance programmes. Admission of normal children to ashram schools would provide a cultural mix.

Seventy-eight student teachers enrolled in the teacher certification program at Fordham University completed three measures of personality, creativity, and classroom perceptions. Person correlations and path analyses were used to analyze the data.

Results indicated that student teachers who maintained a student-centered classroom focus tended to have high needs for affiliation and endurance, with low needs for cognitive structure, aggression, and harm avoidance. These same individuals also evidenced high scores on measures of creativity. More creative student teachers tended to have low needs for social recognition and structure. Five path models were generated based upon the pattern of inter-correlations obtained.

Although personality and creativity were found to have some significant direct effects on classroom focus, personality was not found to have an indirect effect mediated by any of the creativity variables. The independent variables accounted for between 10% and 22% of the variance in classroom focus, indicating the need to consider additional variables for inclusion in future studies in order to improve the predictive power of the model.

Hieberger (1983), on a sample of elementary school students studied about the effects of two Creativity Training Programmes upon the Creativity and Achievement of Young, Intellectually gifted student. Guilford's structure of Intellect (SI) model which was designed in 1959 has been utilized in the study of creativity. Analysis of data using tests and Analysis of covariance revealed that students in Creativity Programme A experienced greater gain than did-students in Creativity Programme B. The achievement level decreased on both sub tests.

Scott (1984) investigated into the influence of Home environment on the development of Creativity in third through fifth grade children. The Problem under investigation was to determine how the home environments of the more creative and less creative child differ. To identify the elements in the home environment that may relate to the child's creativity. To determine the correlation between the home environment and Creativity, mothers of the children tested were administered a 150 questions interview schedule. The results showed that creative children were found differ from non-creative children at a statistically significant level in three areas, variety of intellectual / cultural activities in the home extent of the child's creative activities and flexibility in the household.

Orieux (1989) on a sample 157 grade eleven students (81 males and 76 females) studies about correlated of Creative Ability and Performance. Creative Ability was assessed with the Wallach kongan divergent thinking tests and Creative performance was assessed from three sources: the creative Activities Checklist (Runeo and Albeert 1985), completed by students. The teacher's Evaluation of students' Creativity and the Parent's Evaluation of Student's Creativity. Correctional analysis were conducted to determine the relationship of the creativity measures with intellectual ability, assessed with a group intelligence test and academic achievement obtained from school records data. The major findings were performances were significantly related to intellectual ability and academic achievement at moderate to low levels. Multivariate analyses of variance conducted to evaluate gender effect for all measures reveled that females significantly differ from males. Females obtaining higher mean scores on two achievement measures.

Howell (1990) studied the relationship between Arts education and Creativity among High School Students. The purpose of the study was to examine possible difference between mean creativity scores of subjects, from High Schools with varying arts education experience, Arts disciplines and degree of Academic Achievement. The tool employed for data collection was Torrance Test of Creative Thinking (TTCT). Analysis of data using one way and two-way ANOVAs revealed that three were tendencies for subjects with the highest TTCT scores to have the highest academic achievement scores. A female in all arts disciplines to score higher than males on TTCT.

Onenye, (1991) investigated into the relationship between the cognitive dimensions of Creativity and Future Time Perspective (FTP). The purpose of the study was to investigate the relationship between the cognitive dimensions of creativity and Future Time Perspective. An attempt was made to investigate Guilford's cognitive model of Creativity with Nurmi's problem solving model of Future Time Perspective. The sample consisted of 135 female Under Graduate Students between the ages 18024. Tools administrated were Guildford's Consequences for measuring Creativity and Future Problem Solving Tasks instrument. The findings were consequences and Future Problem Solving Tasks were significantly correlated on all the creativity variables considered. Creativity was found to be stronger predictor of future time Perspective than academic achievement.

Kin (1993) studied the relationship of creativity measures to School Achievement and Preferred Learning and Thinking Style in a sample of 193 Korean High School Students. The Creativity constructs were operationalized in terms of scores on selected measures taken from the Torrance Test of Creative Thinking (TTCT). The statistical techniques used Person's Product moment Correlation Coefficients, t-tests and Analysis of Variance. The major findings were measures of Creativity translated from the Torrance Test of Creative Thinking (TTCT) show little, in any, relationship to School achievement. Korean High School females may be expected to exhibit higher average levels of performance on creativity tests than their male counter parts.

Bisset (1996) investigated into the relationship of Creativity and Achievement to performance of middle School students in solving real world science problems. Tools administered on a sample of fourteen groups of seventh-grade students were the Torrance Creative Problem Solving Figural Test and California Achievement Test. Analysis of data revealed that both creativity and achievement and indicators of success in-group problem solving of ill-structured problems. Creativity reflected greater significance than group achievement on the California Achievement test, as an indicator of success in problem solving on the undersea city Design problem.

Baues Ann Leslie (1995) investigated "Helping children to Maturity Measuring the effect of participation in a pear facilitation project on sixth graders self-esteem, social maturity and patterns of social choice." This research explored the question whether the affective benefits associates with participating in peer facilitation can be empirically measured. Much of the literature concerning peer facilitation can be empirically measured. Much of the literature concerning peer facilitation has discussed the affective benefits of participation and proposed theoretical explanations for those benefits. The most common kind of support for those claims has been anecdotal in nature.

The population chosen for the study was rural mainstream sixth grade students. They were divided into a control group (N=9) and treatment groups. Treatment group 1 (N=30) had high school student group leaders and Treatment group 2 (N=25) had adult group leaders. The sixth grades were trained for 10 weeks in active listening skills and then matched with kindergarten students completed 15 development pay lessons.

Pre and post measurements were collected concerning self-esteem Rosonberg self Esteem Scale, (1965). Interpersonal development skills - Beset and Palomares, (1970). Socio-metric patterns of choice - COMPSOC Tread well and Saxton, (1993). "T" tests were calculated to determine changes by group and by gender. Significant results were found for self-esteem and for some choice patterns.

Results for interpersonal skills were unclear and some choice patterns were not affected. In addition adult professional group leadership was found to be more beneficial than group leadership. Some significant differences were found for gender. Several sub-hypothesis were tested involving the relationship between self-esteem popularity and empathy and some significant results were found. Socio-grams were drawn pre and post for each group and the implications of the patterns that emerged were discussed at the Marco and Micro level.

STUDIES ON SOCIAL MATURITY

Indian Studies

GHOSH. S (1975) studied the social maturity of per school age Bengali children of Calcutta city belonging to different socio-economic groups. The major objectives where to construct a scale for the appraisal of social maturity. To determine social maturity on the basis of the social quotient distribution of the sample concerned. To certify the value of social quotient in predicting the intelligence quotient. To apply the scale for appraisal of social maturity of normal (longitudinal study) and different clinical groups.

Sings of age wise social growth and the characteristic pattern of behaviour expressing age wise social maturity were studied and on the basis of the findings, a scale for the appraisal of Social maturity, viz., a Social Maturity Inventory was constructed.

Thirty-six, nursery and kindergarten schools were randomly selected from the different regions of Calcutta and 40 pre-school children (20 boys and 20 Girls) were selected ROM each school at random equally distributed in each age group. Data were also collected by using a standardized interview schedule on the mother of these selected children. The final sample included 1410 cases.

Social age scores and social quotients (SQ) were found out for all the children. The reliability, predictability validity and norms for the inventory were established. The capacity of the scale for the clientele was testified. Possible deviations were determined. Influential modes that might affect the growth sign of social behavior and there by the social quotient of a child were looked for. The study revealed that sex had very insignificant as testimony of ability to enrich the social maturity level. Social competency was the consequence of acculturation feedback, irrespective of any training or controlled environment. The instrument was highly reliable and valid. The derived equation for determining social maturity was found.

Agnihotri, C.S. (1991) has conducted a cross cultural comparative study between tribal and non tribal first generation and traditional learners in relation to their social maturity and educational adjustment. The sample consisted of 113 first generation tribal learners and 108 traditional tribal learners. Social maturity was independent of traditions of learning. The tribal and non-tribal differed in terms of their placements on attribute of social maturity. The traditions of learning were found to be contributing to social maturity. It was found that, the social maturity and educational adjustment were only social ingredients. Psychological characteristics also influenced the social ingredients. Psychological characteristics also influenced the social maturity and educational adjustment of children and social maturity was independent of traditions of learning.

Bhushan, A. (1994) conducted a study on social maturity across sex and family vocations. The sample comprised of 200 student teachers from two colleges, equally divided between two sexes. Major variable used were sex values, and family vocations. The tools used for data collections were the form D of value survey. The study highlights, male and female uniformly assigned highest importance to social maturity. Both male and female from service and non-service class had politeness as a subdivision on their maturity.

Puranki, S.D (1985) investigated the relationship of social maturity of pupils with organizational climate and Teacher's morale in the primary schools of Bangalore city. The study was conducted to find out the levels of social maturity of male and female students separately. The levels of social maturity of male and female students separately. The levels of social maturity of students under the influence of selected independent variables. The relationship between social maturity of students on the one hand and organizational climate and morale of teachers on the other. Morale of male and female teachers separately. Morale of teachers under different variables. The sample of the study included 70 schools 2634 students and 712 teachers.

The tools used for the study were Thirtha's social maturity scale, Sharma's organizational climate Descriptive Questionnaire and the Teacher's Morale scale designed by the investigator. The statistical techniques used were one-way ANOVA, co-efficient of correlation and 't' test.

The major findings were that the social maturity level of female students was higher than that of male students. In the development of social maturity, autonomous climate, private management and unaided schools and urban location of schools were found to be most conductive factors. The morale of female teachers was higher than that of male teachers. The controlled organizational climate, government, management and urban locality were conductive to development of morale of teachers. No single dimension of organizational climate was effective for the development of social maturity of students. Morale of all teachers who formed the subjects of study was found to be non-effective in contributing to the development of social maturity of their students. No effect of morale of teachers of both sexes was noticed on the development of social maturity of male of female students or on the students of both sexes even under the influence of organizational climates, school organizations and localities.

Foreign Studies

Pattramon Jumpangern (1986) studied the Social Maturity of Teachers-college students of western region of Thailand, in the context of some psycho-socio factors.

The major objectives were to prepare a reliable and valid tool to measure social maturity. To study the social maturity of teacher-college students of the western region of Thailand coming from urban and rural areas. To study the social maturity of teacher-college students of different sex. To study the social maturity of the teachers-college students of different age groups. To study the social maturity of the teachers-college students in the context of their SES. To study the social maturity of the teachers-college students in the context of certain personality trains namely, Dominance Vs Submission, Leadership, Radicalism Vs Conventionalism, Neuroticism, Emotional Stability and Suggestibility. To study the social maturity of student teachers in relation to their personal, social and family adjustment.

For collecting the data for maturity the researcher constructed a social maturity scale by following the mixed model technique. Initially 95 statements were constructed keeping in view the behavior of socially matured individuals. Our of these statements, by applying various techniques of item discrimination. 60 statements were selected for final from. The age norms were established over a sample 669. The reliability of the scale established by various methods ranged between 0.78 and 0.92. The concept and concurrent validity were established. The other tools used for collecting data were SES by A.A. Patel and Personality Inventory by A.S. Patel.

For studying social in relation to certain personality traits, a 2*2*3 factorial design was used. Analysis of variance was used for verifying the hypotheses.

The teachers - college students coming from urban areas were found to be more matured than those coming from rural areas. The male student teachers were found superior to the female student teachers. The student teachers of age group 25-29 were more matured than student teacher of age group 17-20 and 21-24. The student teachers with high SES were more socially matured than those low SES. Students with dominance personality traits were more socially matured than those having submissive personality traits. Students have high leaderships traits were more socially matured than those having low leadership traits. "Students having radicalism personality traits were more socially matured than those having conventionalist traits. Students having low neuroticism were socially matured than those having high neuroticism.

Students having emotional stability were more matured than those having low emotional stability. Students having good family adjustment were more socially matured than those having poor family adjustment. Students having good personal adjustment were more socially matured than those having poor personnel social adjustment.

Banes Ann Leslie (1995) conducted a study on measuring of effect of participation in a peer facilitation project on sixth graders self esteem, social maturity and patterns of social choice. The population chosen for the study was rural mainstream sixth grade students. The sample was tested by Socimetric pattern of choice. It was found that some significant difference in social maturity for gender and there was significant relationship between self-esteem and social maturity.

Savluk Thongngamkahom., (1983) studied the social maturity as a function of some psycho-socio adjustments factors of B.Ed., college students of North-central region f Thailand. The major objectives were to prepare a reliable and valid to measure social maturity. To study the social maturity of B.Ed., college students in the North-Central region of Thailand. To study the Social Maturity of B.Ed., college students coming from single sex schools and mixed schools. To compare Social Maturity of B.Ed., college students of different sexes. To study the Social Maturity of B.Ed., college students with regard to their socio-economic status. To study the social Maturity of B.Ed., college students with regard to their socio-economic status. To study the Social Maturity in relation to personal social adjustment. To study the Social Maturity in relation to family adjustment.

The sample of the study included 922 students, including boys and girls from the North-Central region. The social maturity scale was prepared by following the Likert method. The scale was standardized on a sample of 922 students, including boys and girls from the North-Central region. The reliability, validity and norms of the scale were established. For measuring SES and personality traits. A.S/Patel's SES scale and personality inventory were translated into English and that were used for collecting the data. The reliability of the scale, as established by different method ranged between 0.84 and 0.92. The concurrent validity established by correlating the scores on the scale with teacher's opinion about maturity was found to be 0.73. The 2x2x2 factorial design and analysis of variance technique was used for arriving at conclusion.

The major findings were that the B.Ed., college students with high SES background were found more socially matured that those of coming from low SES strata. The students having dominant personality trait were more socially matured than those of having submissive personality trait. The students having high leadership personality trait were more socially matured than those of having low leadership personality trait. The students having radicalism personality trait were more socially matured than those having conventionalist personality trait. The students having low neuroticism were more socially matured than those having high neuroticism. The students having high emotional maturity were more socially matured than those having suggestibility and low suggestibility traits neither did nor differ on social maturity. The students having good social adjustment were more socially matured than those having poor personal social adjustment. The students having good family adjustment were found to be more socially matured than those with poor family adjustment.

CONCLUSION

From the above description of the creativity and social maturity, the investigator has understood the need for the full-fledged studies on creativity and social maturity. In most of the studies the researchers used the standardized tools only. From the analysis it has been found that there is no study related to creativity and social maturity was conducted. Social maturity and creativity are very much needed for the teacher trainees. So the investigator has selected this topic for his research work.

❒

13

Methodology

Research is always directed towards solution to some problems. It develops the curiosity about the unknown and it is a procedure from known to unknown. The ultimate goal of any research work is to find out the cause and effect relationship between the variables. Educational research is concerned with the development and testing theories of how students behave in the educational setting. The success of an educational research depends on the systematic adoption of the scientific method. A research process so implemented would enhance the validity and reliability of the research.

RESEARCH METHODS

A research method is a systematic process of collecting and analyzing Information (data) for some purpose. Researchers use different methods in their research activities. The selection of such method depends on the nature, objectives and population of the study. John. W. Best (1977) says, "Research is a more systematic activity directed towards discovery and the development of an organized body of knowledge" (P-308) Educational researchers generally use methods such as survey research, experimental research, historical research, ethnographic research and comparative research.

HYPOTHESES

1. There is a significant difference in the fluency level between men and women teacher trainees.

2. There is a significant difference in the flexibility level between men and women teacher trainees.
3. There is a significant difference in the originality level between men and women teacher trainees.
4. There is a significant difference in the personal adequacy between men and women teacher trainees.
5. There is a significant difference in the interpersonal adequacy between men and women teacher trainees.
6. There is a significant difference in the social adequacy between men and women teacher trainees.
7. There is a significant difference in the social maturity between men and women teacher trainees.
8. There is a significant difference between teacher trainees studying in Government and Aided Institutions with respect to fluency level.
9. There is a significant difference between teacher trainees studying in Government and Either Institutions with respect to flexibility level.
10. There is a significant difference between teacher trainees studying in Government and Aided Institutions with respect to originality level.
11. There is a significant difference between teacher trainees studying in Government and Aided Institutions with respect to personal adequacy on social maturity.
12. There is a significant difference between teacher trainees studying in Government and Aided Institutions with respect to Interpersonal adequacy on social maturity.
13. There is a significant difference between teacher trainees studying in Government and Aided Institutions with respect to social adequacy on social maturity.
14. There is a significant difference between teacher trainees studying in Government and Aided Institutions with respect to social maturity.
15. There is a significant difference between teacher trainees studying in first year and second year with respect to fluency level on creativity.
16. There is a significant difference between teacher trainees studying in first year and second year with respect to flexibility level on creativity.
17. There is a significant difference between teacher trainees studying in first year and second year with respect to originality level on creativity.
18. There is a significant difference between teacher trainees studying in first year and second year with respect to personal adequacy on social maturity scale.
19. There is a significant difference between teacher trainees studying in first year and second year with respect to interpersonal adequacy on social maturity scale.

20. There is a significant difference between teacher trainees studying in first year and second year with respect to Social adequacy on social maturity scale.
21. There is a significant difference between teacher trainees studying in first year and second year with respect to social maturity scale.
22. There is a significant difference between teacher trainees of the creativity factors based on their father's qualifications.
23. There is a significant difference between teacher trainees of the social maturity based on their father's qualifications.
24. There is a significant difference between teacher trainees of the creativity factors based on their mother's qualifications.
25. There is a significant difference between teacher trainees of the social maturity based on their mother's qualifications.
26. There is a significant difference between teacher trainees of the creativity factors based on their parental income.
27. There is a significant difference between teacher trainees of the social maturity based on their Parental Income.
28. There is significant relationship between creativity dimensions and personal adequacy of teacher trainees.
29. There is significant relationship between creativity dimensions and interpersonal adequacy of teacher trainees.
30. There is significant relationship between creativity dimensions and social adequacy of teacher trainees.
31. There is significant relationship between creativity dimensions and social maturity of teacher trainees.

TOOLS SELECTED FOR THE PRESENT STUDY

The study aims at studying the creative thinking and social maturity of Secondary Grade teacher Trainees. For measuring the investigator had used the Verbal Test for Creative Thinking prepared and standardized by Baqer Mehdi, (1973).

Description of the Verbal Test

The Verbal test of creativity includes four sub tests namely consequences test, unusual test, new relationship test and product improvement test.

1. Consequences test

The consequences tests consist of three hypothetical situations. A) What would happen if man could fly like birds? B) What would happen if our college had wheels? C) What would happen if man does not have any need for food?

Their subject is required to think as many consequences of these situations as he can and write them under each situation in the space provided. The situations being hypothetical minimize the effects of experiences and also provide the subject with an unlimited opportunity to make responses. The test encourages free play of imagination and originality. An example is given on the test booklet to acquaint the subjects with the nature of the test. The time allowed for the three problems is 4 minutes each.

2. Unusual Test

This test presents the subjects with the names of three common objects and requires him to write as many novel, interesting and unusual uses of these objects as he may think of. The example given on the test booklet properly acquaints the subjects with the nature of the task. The test measures the subjects ability to retrieve items of information from his personal information in storage. Evidently, it measures also the subjects ability to shift frames of reference to use the environment in an original manner. The time allowed for the three tasks is 5 minutes each.

3. New-Relationship test

This test presents the subject with three pairs of words apparently different tree and house chair and ladder, air and water and requires him to think and write as many novel relationship as possible between the two objects of each pair in the space provided. The test provides an opportunity for the free play of imagination and originality. The time allowed for each pair of words is 5 minutes.

4. Product improvement test

In this test; the subject is asked to think of simple wooden toy of horse and suggest addition of new things to it to make it more interesting for the children to play. The time allowed is 6 minutes.

The total time required for administering the test is 48 minutes in addition to the time necessary for giving instruction, passing out test booklets to children and collecting them back.

RELIABILITY OF THE TEST

The test-retest reliabilities of the factor scores and also the Total score were obtained on a small sample (N-50). Test-retest reliabilities of Factor scores and Total creativity score.

TABLE. 13.1: Reliability coefficient of the creativity test

Fluency	Flexibility	Originality
0.945	0.921	0.896

It may be seen that both the factor score and total creativity score reliabilities are considerably high ranging from 0.896 to 0.945. These values are highly satisfactory. The reliability of the total score, which come out to be 927, is again quite high. Inter scorer reliabilities, for the factor scores in one study were found to range from 653 to 981.

VALDITY OF THE TEST

The Validity co-efficient for each factor are given in table. The index of Validity is the square toot of reliability and is given in the table 3.02

TABLE. 1 3.2:

Fluency	Flexibility	Originality
0.97	0.96	0.95

All correlations are significant beyond .01 levels. The validity coefficient for factor scores and the total creativity score are high enough to place confidence in the use of the test.

POPULATION AND SAMPLE

The study is related to creative thinking of Secondary grade teacher trainees studying in Chennai city.

(i) SAMPLE

225 teacher trainees were taken for the study of which 124 students are from Government teacher training institutes and 101 from Government teacher training institutes. The sampling techniques used were stratified random sampling.

TABLE. 13.3: Institutions Sellected for the Study

S. No	Name of the Institution	No of sample
1.	DIET at Chennai	124
2.	Christopher Teacher Training Institute, Chennai	101

TABLE. 13.4: Distribution of Sample Based on Gender

Gender	Grequency	Percentage
Men	125	55.6
women	100	44.4
Total	**225**	**100**

TABLE. 13.5: Distribution of Sample Based on Type of Management

Management	Frequency	Percentage
Government	124	55.6
Aided	101	44.4
Total	**225**	**100**

ADMINISTRATION OF THE BEST

The test administer first gets himself acquainted with the test by carefully going through the test booklet, which contains the general, instructions and instructions and instructions for each activity. The timings given for each activity adhered to.

1. The place for administering the test was such that the teacher trainees may work comfortably and without disturbance. The usual setting for the test administration is in the classroom. The pupils were properly motivated to take the test the language used by the administrator in giving institutions to children was as simple as possible so that each one understands what is required of him. The test administrator had a stopwatch nothing the timing for each activity.

PROCEDURE FOR SCORING

As there is no right or wrong response for the test much care has to be exercised at the time of scoring and the use of scoring sheet. Each item is to be scored for fluency, flexibility and originality. The scoring procedure is given below.

(i) Fluency

Fluency is represented by the number of relevant and unrepeated ideas which the tester produces. Relevance is judged to the basis of the appropriateness of the response when considered in relation to the test problem. An unrepeated idea is one which has been expressed only once under a given problem.

(ii) Flexibility

Flexibility is represented by a person's ability to produce ideas, which differ in approach or thought trend. All ideas which fall under one category of though trend are treated as one for purpose of flexibility scoring. Thus is five ideas are produced and all belong to only one category of approach, flexibility will be one but if all the five ideas are based on five different approaches or thought trends, then the flexibility score will be five.

(iii) Originality

Originality is represented by uncommonness of a given response. The uncommon the response the higher the originality werights.

SOCIAL MATURITY SCALE

To study the Social Maturity of secondary grade teacher-trainees the SMS (Social Maturity Scale) designed and Standardized by Dr. Nalini Rao Ph.D was selected and used.

RELIABILITY AND VALIDITY OF THE TEST

In order to establish the reliability of the Social Maturity Scale the odd-even method was used. Pilot study was conducted among fifty secondary grade teacher trainees. The reliability coefficient was computed by using Spearman's formula to be 0.87. The intrinsic validity was found to be 0.93. Hence the Social Maturity Scale was selected for the study.

COLLECTION OF DATA

As planned earlier the Investigator approached the head of the Institutions with the appraisal of the research programme. The social maturity scale was administered to the students in groups in the regular class room situation with the help of the teachers in change of the teacher trainees. The investigator gave the instruction to the teacher trainees so as to ensure better co-operation and get their responses objectively. The time allowed to complete the scale items was one hour.

SCORING

Nearly fifty percent of the items on each sub scale were worded in the Positive direction and the other half were negatively oriented. Thus the positively oriented statements had their "mature" in the disagreement direction. The scale points on the intervals were subsequently scored 4,3,2,1 for all the positive items where the highest score represented the most mature response and the negative items where the highest scored in the reversed order. Among the 90 items the positive statements are 17, 21, 24, 26, 36, 39, 41, 50, 51, 52, 54,

57, 63, 74, 80, 83, 86, 87 and 90. The remaining were the negative statements. The scoring was done according to the scoring key given in the manual.

STATISTICAL TECHNIQUES USED

Research dispends on statistics. When descriptions are quantified they can be analyzed well. Statistical techniques must be familiar with basic statistical procedure, their limitations in usage and the areas of their application. These procedures help to find the estimates of the population. The investigator has planned to use the following statistical techniques for the analysis of data.

Suitable descriptive and inferential statistical techniques were used in the interpretation of the data to draw our more meaningful picture of results from the collected data. In the present study following statistical measures were used.

(a) Mean

$$A = \frac{\sum fd}{\sum f} xi$$

(b) Standard Deviation

$$SD = \sigma \sqrt{\frac{\sum fd}{N} - \left[\frac{\sum fd}{N}\right]^2}$$

(c) Standard error of mean deviation

$$SEMD = \sqrt{\frac{\sigma_2^2}{N_1} 1 + \frac{\sigma_2^2}{N_2}}$$

(d) Critical Ratio

(e) Correlation Coefficient (r)

$$C.R = \frac{{}^{N}\sum xy - \sum x \sum y}{\left({}^{N}\sum x - (\sum x)^2 (N\sum y - (\sum y)\right)^2}$$

(f) F - ratio

$$F\text{- ratio} = \frac{Variance\ between\ group}{Varicane\ within\ group}$$

CONCLUSTION

This chapter outlines the design of the present study, the procedure followed and the nature of the sample. It describes the hypotheses to be tested, the tool used and the methods of administration and scoring. The method of investigation designed and followed was found to be quite appropriate and effective for the study.

❒

14

Analysis of the Data

According to Wilkinson and Bhandarkar (1987), analysis of data involves a number of closely related operations that are performed with the purpose of summarizing the collected data and organizing these in such a manner that will yield answer to research question or suggest hypotheses or questions if no such questions hypothesis had initiated the study.

This chapter focuses on statistical analysis to test the hypotheses framed in this study and report of the obtained findings in interpreted. The influence of social maturity on creativity was analysed using appropriate statistics. The same was also analysed considering the background variables namely gender, type of the institution, parental education and year of study. The statistical techniques were mean, standard deviation, t-ratio ANOVA and coefficients of correlations were used.

TESTING OF HYPOTHESIS

HYPOTHESIS - 1

There is a significant difference in the fluency level between men and women teacher trainees

TABLE. 14.1: Difference between fluency level of men and women teacher trainees

Creativity	Gender	N	Mean	S.D	S.E.M.	t-ratio	L.S
Fluency	Male	125	16.66	8.860	0.79	1.12	N.S
	Female	100	17.94	8.079	0.81		

INTERPRETATION

From the above table it is observed that the mean scores obtained for the men and women teacher trainees for fluency level of creativity shows that female member scores higher than the male teacher trainees. But it is not statistically proved and hence the empirical hypothesis is not proved.

HYPOTHESIS - 2

There is a significant difference in the flexibility level between men and women teacher trainees

TABLE.14.2: Difference Between Flexibility Level of Men and Women Teacher Trainees

Creativity	Gender	N	Mean	S.D	S.E.M.	t-ratio	L.S
Flexibity	Male	125	15.93	8.424	0.75	2.34	0.05
	Female	100	18.35	6.746	0.68		

INTERPREATION

From the above table it is observed that the mean scores obtained for the men and women teacher trainees for flexibility level of creativity shows that female member scores higher than the male teacher trainees. But it neither is nor statistically proved that there is a significant difference at 0.05 levels hence the empirical hypothesis is retained.

HYPOTHESIS - 3

There is a significant difference in the originality level between men and women teacher trainees

TABLE. 14.3: Differences Between Originality Livel of Men and Women Teacher Trainees

Creativity	Gender	N	Mean	S.D	S.E.M.	t-ratio	L.S
Originality	Male	125	18.86	7.326	0.66	2.94	0.01
	Female	100	15.85	7.921	0.80		

INTERPREATION

From the above table it is observed that the mean scores obtained for the men and women teacher trainees for fluency level of originality level of creativity shows that female member scores higher than the male teacher trainees. It is also statistically proved to be significant at 0.01 level and hence the empirical hypothesis is retained.

HYPOTHESIS - 4

There is a significant difference in the personal adequacy between men and women teacher trainees

TABLE. 14.4: Differences Between Personal Adequancy of Men and Women Teacher Trainees

Creativity	Gender	N	Mean	S.D	S.E.M.	t-ratio	L.S
Personal Adequacy	Male	125	98.86	34.44	3.08	1.180	N.S
	Female	100	99.72	25.30	2.53		

INTERPREATION

From the above table it is observed that the mean scores obtained for the men and women teacher trainees for the personal adequacy of social ma shows that female member scores higher than the male teacher trainees. But the difference is not significant and hence the empirical hypothesis is rejected.

HYPOTHESIS - 5

There is a significant difference in the interpersonal adequacy between men and women teacher trainees

TABLE. 14.5: Differences Between Interpersonal Adequacy of Men and Women Teacher Trainees

Creativity	Gender	N	Mean	S.D	S.E.M.	t-ratio	L.S
Interpersonal Adequacy	Male	125	108.03	28.45	2.54	1.694	N.S
	Female	100	107.53	24.73	2.47		

INTERPREATION

From the above table it is observed that the mean scores obtained for the men and women teacher trainees for the interpersonal adequacy of social maturity shows that female member scores higher than the male teacher trainees. But it is not statistically proved. Hence the empirical hypothesis is rejected.

HYPOTHESIS - 6

There is a significant difference in the social adequacy between men and women teacher trainees

TABLE. 14.6: Differences Between Social Adequacy ofMen and Women Teacher Trainees

Creativity	Gender	N	Mean	S.D	S.E.M.	t-ratio	L.S
Social adequacy	Male	125	98.40	28.59	2.55	1.033	N.S
	Female	100	94.17	32.75	3.28		

INTERPREATION

From the above table it is observed that the mean scores obtained for the men and women teacher trainees for Social adequacy of social maturity shows that male member scores higher than the female teacher trainees. It is also statistically not proved and thus the empirical hypothesis is rejected.

HYPOTHESIS - 7

There is a significant difference in the social maturity between men and women teacher trainees

TABLE. 14.7: Differences Between Social Maturity of Men and Women Teacher Trainees

Creativity	Gender	N	Mean	S.D	S.E.M.	t-ratio	L.S
Social maturity	Male	125	305.32	52.93	4.73	1.712	N.S
	Female	100	334.42	80.65	8.06		

INTERPREATION

From the above table it is observed that the mean scores obtained for the men and women teacher trainees for fluency level of social maturity shows that female member scores higher than the male teacher trainees. But the difference in means is not significant. Hence the empirical hypothesis is rejected.

HYPOTHESIS - 8

There is a significant difference between teacher trainees studying in Government and Aided Institutions with respect to fluency level.

TABLE.14.8: Difference Between Fluency Level of Teacher Trainees Studying in Government and Aided Institutions

Creativity	Institution	N	Mean	S.D	S.E.M.	t-ratio	L.S
Fluency	Government	125	17.15	8.719	0.167	0.167	N.S.
	Govt.aided	100	17.34	8.326	0.828		

INTERPREATION

From the above table it is observed that the mean scores obtained for the fluency level of teacher trainees studying in Government vs. Aided institutions on the creativity show little difference on their fluency level and is not significant at any level. Hence the empirical hypothesis is not proved.

HYPOTHESIS - 9

There is a significant difference between teacher trainees studying in Government and Aided Institutions with respect to flexibility level.

TABLE. 14.9: Difference Between Flexibility Level of Teacher Trainees Studyubg ub Giverbnebt abd Auded Ubstutytuibs

Creativity	Institution	N	Mean	S.D	S.E.M.	t-ratio	L.S
Flexibility	Government	125	17.98	7.953	0.714	2.085	0.05
	Govt.aided	100	15.81	7.478	0.744		

INTERPREATION

From the above table it is observed that the mean scores obtained for the flexibility level of teacher trainees studying in Government vs. Aided institutions on the creativity show than the teacher trainees studying in the Government institutions have more flexibility level that the aided institutions. The difference is means is found to be significant at 0.05 level and hence the hypothesis is retained.

HYPOTHESIS - 10

There is a significant difference between teacher trainees studying in Government and Aided Institutions with respect to originality level.

TABLE. 14.10: Difference Between Originality Level of Teacher Trainees Studying in Government and Aided Institution

Creativity	Institution	N	Mean	S.D	S.E.M.	t-ratio	L.S
Flexibility	Government	125	16.68	7.712	0.695	1.814	N.S
	Govt.aided	100	18.55	7.650	0.761		

INTERPREATION

From the above table it is observed that the mean scores obtained for the originality level of teacher trainees studying in Government vs. Aided institutions on the creativity show difference on their originality level. But it is not statistically proved and hence the empirical hypothesis is not proved.

HYPOTHESIS - 11

There is a significant difference between teacher trainees studying in Government and Aided Institutions with respect to personal adequacy on social maturity.

TABLE. 14.11: Difference Between Personal Adequacy of Teacher Trainees Studying in Government and Aided Institutions

Creativity	Institution	N	Mean	S.D	S.E.M.	t-ratio	L.S
personal adequacy	Government	125	100.51	25.03	2.331	0.850	NS
	Govt.aided	100	99.54	28.07	2.793		

INTERPREATION

From the above table it is observed that the mean scores obtained for the personal adequacy of teacher trainees studying in Government and Aided institutions on social maturity shows that trainees studying in Government institutions scores higher than the teacher trainees studying in aided institutions. But is not statistically not proved and hence the empirical hypothesis is rejected.

HYPOTHESIS - 12

There is a significant difference between teacher trainees studying in Government and Aided Institutions with respect to interpersonal adequacy on social maturity.

TABLE. 14.12: Difference Between Interpersonal Adequacy of Teacher Trainees Studying in Government and Aided Institutions

Creativity	Institution	N	Mean	S.D	S.E.M.	t-ratio	L.S
Interpersonal adequacy	Government	125	105.31	27.84	2.500	2.216	0.05
	Govt.aided	100	107.67	23.71	2.310		

INTERPREATION

From the above table it is observed that the mean scores obtained for the interpersonal adequacy of teacher trainees studying in Government and Aided institutions on social maturity shows that trainees studying in Government aided institutions scores higher than the teacher trainees studying in Government institutions. This is statistically proved and found to be significant at 0,05 level and hence the empirical hypothesis is retained.

HYPOTHESIS - 13

There is a significant difference between teacher trainees studying in Government and Aided Institutions with respect to social adequacy on social maturity.

TABLE. 14.13: Difference Between Social Adequacy of Teacher Trainees Studying in Government and Aided Institutions

Creativity	**Institution**	**N**	**Mean**	**S.D**	**S.E.M.**	**t-ratio**	**L.S**
Social adequacy	Government	125	106.50	29.05	2.610	5.821	0.01
	Govt.aided	100	104.27	27.78	2.765		

INTERPREATION

From the above table it is observed that the mean scores obtained for the social adequacy of teacher trainees studying in Government vs. Aided institutions on social maturity shows that trainees studying in Government institutions scores higher than the teacher trainees studying in aided institutions.

The difference in means is statistically proved to be significance and hence the empirical hypothesis is retained.

HYPOTHESIS - 14

There is a significant difference between teacher trainees studying in Government and Aided Institutions with respect to social maturity.

TABLE. 14.14: Difference Between Social Maturity of Teacher Trainees Studying in Government and Aided Institutions

Creativity	Institution	N	Mean	S.D	S.E.M.	t-ratio	L.S
Social maturity	Government	125	312.32	23.59	4.45	2.02	0.05
	Govt.aided	100	318.48	22.05	4.85		

INTERPREATION

From the above table it is observed that the mean scores obtained for the social maturity teacher trainees studying in Government vs. Aided institutions on social maturity shows that trainees studying in Government aided institutions scores higher than the teacher trainees studying in Government institutions. It is statistically not proved and hence the empirical hypothesis is rejected.

HYPOTHESIS - 15

There is a significant difference between teacher trainees studying in first year and second year with respect to fluency level of creativity.

TABLE. 14.15: Difference Between Fluency Level of Teacher Trainees Studying First Year and Second Year

Creativity	Institution	N	Mean	S.D	S.E.M.	t-ratio	L.S
Fluency	Ist Year	112	18.62	7.43	0.70	2.45	0.05
	2nd year	113	15.86	9.31	0.87		

INTERPREATION

From the above table it is observed that the mean scores obtained for the first year and second year teacher trainees for fluency level of creativity shows that first year students scores higher than the second year teacher trainees. It is statistically proved and hence the empirical hypothesis is proved.

HYPOTHESIS - 16

There is a significant difference between teacher trainees studying in first year and second year with respect to flexibility level of creativity.

TABLE. 14.16: Differences Between Flexibility Level of Teacher Trainees Studying First Year and Seocnd Year

Creativity	Institution	N	Mean	S.D	S.E.M.	t-ratio	L.S
Flexibility	I[st] Year	112	16.82	7.81	0.73	0.35	NS
	2nd year	113	17.19	7.81	0.73		

INTERPREATION

From the above table it is observed that the mean scores obtained for the first year and second year teacher trainees for flexibility level of creativity shows that second year students scores higher than the first year teacher trainees. It is statistically not proved and hence the empirical hypothesis is not proved.

HYPOTHESIS - 17

There is a significant difference between teacher trainees studying in first year and second year with respect to originality level on creativity.

TABLE. 14.17: Differences Between Originality Level of Teacher Trainees Studying First Year and Second Year

Creativity	Institution	N	Mean	S.D	S.E.M.	t-ratio	L.S
Originality	I[st] Year	112	17.38	7.71	0.72	0.29	N.S
	2nd year	113	17.68	7.77	0.73		

INTERPREATION

From the above table it is observed that the mean scores obtained for the first year and second year teacher trainees for originality level of creativity shows that not much difference between first year and second year teacher trainees. Hence the empirical hypothesis is not proved.

HYPOTHESIS - 18

There is a significant difference between teacher trainees studying in first year and second year with respect to fluency level of creativity.

TABLE. 14.18: Differences Between Personal Adequacy of Teacher Trainees Studying First Year and Second Year

Category	Year	N	Mean	S.D	S.E.M.	t-ratio	L.S
Personal Adequacy	I[st] Year	112	103.81	35.15	3.32	0.208	N.S
	2nd year	113	106.25	30.57	3.42		

INTERPREATION

From the above table it is observed that the mean scores obtained for personal adequacy of teacher trainees studying first year and second year on social maturity shows that trainees studying second year scored higher than the teacher trainees studying in first year. It is statistically not paved and hence the empirical hypothesis is rejected.

HYPOTHESIS - 19

There is a significant difference between teacher trainees studying in first year and second year with respect to interpersonal adequacy on social maturity scale.

TABLE. 14.19: Differences Between Interpersonal Adequacy of Teacher Trainees Studying First Year and Second Year

Category	Year	N	Mean	S.D	S.E.M.	t-ratio	L.S
Interpersonal	Ist Year	112	123.86	25.16	2.26	1.243	N.S
Adequacy	2nd year	113	109.60	25.68	2.41		

INTERPREATION

From the above table it is observed that the mean scores obtained for the interpersonal adequacy of teacher trainees studying first year and second year on social maturity shows that trainees studying first year scored higher than the teacher trainees studying in second year. It is statistically proved and hence the empirical hypothesis is rejected.

HYPOTHESIS - 20

There is a significant difference between teacher trainees studying in first year and second year with respect to social adequacy on social maturity scale.

TABLE. 14.20: Difference Between Social Adequacy of Teacher Trainees Studying First Year and Secon Year

Category	Year	N	Mean	S.D	S.E.M.	t-ratio	L.S
Social	Ist Year	112	98.38	32.09	3.03	0.907	N.S
Adequacy	2nd year	113	94.68	28.88	2.72		

INTERPREATION

From the above table it is observed that the mean scores obtained for social adequacy of teacher trainees studying first year and second year on social maturity shows that trainees studying first year scored higher than the teacher trainees studying in second year. It is statistically not proved and hence the empirical hypothesis is rejected.

HYPOTHESIS - 21

There is a significant difference between teacher trainees studying in first year and second year with respect to social maturity scale.

TABLE. 14.21: Differences Between Social Maturity of Teacher Trainees Studying First Year and Second Year

Category	Year	N	Mean	S.D	S.E.M.	t-ratio	L.S
Social	I[st] Year	112	309.04	29.39	7.71	0.41	N.S
Maturity	2nd year	113	310.53	25.12	5.76		

INTERPREATION

From the above table it is observed that the mean scores obtained for social maturity of teacher trainees studying first year and second year on social maturity shows that trainees studying first year scored higher than the teacher trainees studying in second year. It is statistically proved and hence the empirical hypothesis is rejected.

HYPOTHESIS -22

There is a significant difference between the teacher trainees of the creativity factors based on their father's qualifications.

The influence of father's qualification on creativity dimensions has been analysed usind ANOVA and the findings are presented in the table 14.22

TABLE. 14.22: Results of Anova For the Dimension Wise Creativity Factors of Secondary Grade Teacher Trainees and Qualifications of Their Father

Category	Sources of Variation	Sun of Squares	Df	Mean square	F	L.S
Fluency	Between Groups	717.283	5			
	within Groups	15568.609	219	71.409		
	Total	16285.982	224	60.612	1.178	N.S
	Between Groups	402.393	5			
	within Groups	12901.446	218	80.479		
Originality	Total	13303.839	223	59.181	1.360	N.S

From the above table, it is observed that the F value is not significant for the creativity test dimensions of the teacher trainees based on their father's qualifications. So the above empirical hypothesis is rejected.

HYPOTHESIS -23

There is a significant difference between the teacher trainees of the creativity factors based on their father's qualifications.

TABLE. 14.23: Results of Anova for the Social Maturity of Secondary Grade Teacher Trainees and Qualifications of their Father

Category	Sources of Variation	Sun of Squares	Df	Mean square	F	L.S
Personal adequacy	Between Groups within Groups Total	64196.322 1647925.4 1712121.7	5 219 224	12839.264 7524.773	1.706	N.S
Interpers adequach	Between Groups within Groups Total	51813.041 1609758.4 1661571.4	5 219 224	10362.608 7350.495	1.410	N.S
Social adequach	Between Groups within Groups Total	24621.711 206123.45 208586.16	5 219 224	492.542 941.203	0.523	N.S
Social Maturity	Between Groups within Groups Total	115358.16 3510108.4 3635466.6	5 219 224	23071.631 16027.892	1.439	N.S

INTERPRETATION

From the above table, it is observed that the F value is not significant for the overall social maturity and dimensions of the teacher trainees based on their father's qualifications. So the above empirical hypothesis is rejected.

HYPOTHESIS -24

There is a significant difference between the teacher trainees of the creativity factors based on their mother's qualifications.

TABLE. 14.24: Results of Anova For the Dimension Wise Creativity Factors of Secondary Grade Teacher Trainees and Qualifications of their Mother

Category	Sources of Variation	Sun of Squares	Df	Mean square	F	L.S
Fluency	Between Groups within Groups Total	551.936 15734.046 16285.982	5 219 224	110.387 71.845	1.536	N.S
Flexibility	Between Groups within Groups Total	218.524 13412.472 13630.996	5 219 224	43.705 61.244	0.714	N.S

Originality	Between Groups within Groups Total	287.130 13016.709 13303.839	5 218 223	57.426 59.710	0.960	N.S

INTERPRETATION

The influence of father's qualification on creativity dimensions has been analysed using ANOVA and the findings are presented in the table 4.24 from the above table, it is observed that the F value is not significant inferring no significant difference between groups with respect to creativity factor.

HYPOTHESIS -25

There is a significant difference between the teacher trainees of the social maturity based on their mother's qualifications.

TABLE. 14.25: Results of Anova for the Social Maturity of Secondary Grade Teacher Trainees and Qualifications of their Mother

Category	Sources of Variation	Sun of Squares	Df	Mean square	F	L.S
Personal adequacy	Between Groups within Groups Total	45566.538 1666555.21 712121.7	5 219 224	9113.308 7609.841	1.198	N.S
Interprets adequacy	Between Groups within Groups Total	31217.820 1661571.4 1630353.6	5 219 224	6243.564 7444.537	0.839	N.S
Social adequacy	Between Groups within Groups Total	3969.280 204616.88 208586.16	5 218 223	793.858 934.324	0.850	N.S
Social Maturity	Between Groups within Groups Total	69632.865 3555833.7 3625466.6	5 219 224	13926.573 16236.684	0.858	N.S

INTERPRETATION

From the above table, it is observed that the F value is not significant for the overall social maturity and dimensions of the teacher trainees based on their mother's qualifications. So the above empirical hypothesis is rejected.

HYPOTHESIS -26

There is a significant difference between the teacher trainees of the creativity factors based on their parental income.

TABLE. 14.26: Results of Anova for the Dimension Wise Creativity Factors of Secondary Grade Teacher Trainees and Income of the Parents

Category	Sources of Variation	Sun of Squares	Df	Mean square	F	L.S
Fluency	Between Groups within Groups Total	25.717 16260.265 16285.982	2 222 224	12.859 73.244	0.176	N.S
Flexibility	Between Groups within Groups Total	29.399 13601.596 13630.996	2 222 224	14.700 61.268	0.240	N.S
Originality	Between Groups within Groups Total	394.534 12909.305 13303.839	2 222 224	58.15 59.39	0.98	N.S

INTERPRETATION

The influence of parental income on creativity dimensions has been analysed using ANOVA and the findings are presented in the table 4.26 from the above table, it is observed that the F value is not significant among the mean creativity test dimensions of the teachers trainees based on their parental income. So the above empirical hypothesis is rejected.

HYPOTHESIS -27

There is a significant difference between the teacher trainees of the social maturity based on their father's qualifications.

TABLE. 14.25: Results of Anova for the Social Maturity of Secondary Grade Teacher Trainees and Parential Income

Category	Sources of Variation	Sun of Squares	Df	Mean square	F	L.S
Personal adequacy	Between Groups within Groups Total	11677.170 1700444.5 1712121.7	2 222 224	5838.585 7659.660	1.198	N.S

Interprets adequacy	Between Groups within Groups Total	31217.820 1661571.4 1630353.6	2 222 224	9545.868 7398.557	1.290	N.S
Social adequacy	Between Groups within Groups Total	74.461 208511.70 208586.16	2 222 224	37.230 939.242	0.040	N.S
Social Maturity	Between Groups within Groups Total	56404.893 3569061.7 3625466.6	2 222 224	28202.446 16076.854	1.754	N.S

INTERPRETATION

From the above table, it is observed that the F value is not significant among the mean maturity of the teacher trainees based on their parental income. So the above empirical hypothesis is rejected.

HYPOTHESIS - 28

There is significant relationship between creativity dimension and personal adequacy of teacher trainees.

TABLE : 14.28: Correlation Coefficient Between Creativity Dimension and Personal Adequacy of Secondary Grade Teacher Trainees

Category	N	r	L.S
Fluency Vs Personal adequacy	225	0.03	N.S
Flexibility Vs Personal adequacy	225	0.02	N.S
Originality Vs Personal adequacy	225	0.04	N.S

INTERPRETATION

The coefficient of the correlation given in the Table 4.28 indicates no significant relation between creativity factors and personal adequacy of secondary grade teacher trainees. So the above empirical hypothesis is not accepted.

HYPOTHESIS - 29

There is significant relationship between creativity dimension and inter personal adequacy of teacher trainees.

TABLE. 14.29: Correlation Coefficipent Between Breativity Dimension and Interpersonal Adequacy of Secondary Grade Teacher Trainees

Category	N	r	L.S
Fluency Vs Personal adequacy	225	0.07	N.S
Flexibility Vs Personal adequacy	225	0.01	N.S
Originality Vs Personal adequacy	225	0.01	N.S

INTERPRETATION

The coefficient of the correlation given in the Table 4.29 indicates no significant relation between creativity factors and interpersonal adequacy of secondary grade teacher trainees. So the above empirical hypothesis is not accepted.

HYPOTHESIS - 30

There is significant relationship between creativity dimension and social adequacy of teacher trainees.

TABLE.14.28: Correlation Coefficient Between Creativity Dimension and Social Adequacy of Secondary Grade Teacher Trainees

Category	N	r	L.S
Fluency Vs Personal adequacy	225	0.37	N.S
Flexibility Vs Personal adequacy	225	0.02	N.S
Originality Vs Personal adequacy	225	0.06	N.S

INTERPRETATION

The coefficient of the correlation given in the Table 14.30 indicates no significant relation between creativity factors and social adequacy of secondary grade teacher trainees. So the above empirical hypothesis is not accepted.

HYPOTHESIS - 31

There is significant relationship between creativity dimension and social maturity of teacher trainees.

TABLE. 14.28: Correlation Coefficient Between Creativity Dimension and Social Maturity of Secondary Grade Teacher Trainees

Category	N	r	L.S
Fluency Vs Personal adequacy	225	0.08	N.S
Flexibility Vs Personal adequacy	225	0.02	N.S
Originality Vs Personal adequacy	225	0.04	N.S

INTERPRETATION

The coefficient of the correlation given in the Table 4.31 indicates no significant relation between creativity factors and social maturity of secondary grade teacher trainees. So the above empirical hypothesis is not accepted.

CONCLUSION

This Chapter Summaries the analysis of data. Testing of hypothesis description and discussion of the table. A brief report of the research study together with the major findings and conclusion along their educational implication has been presented in the succeeding chapter.

❐

15

Summary of Findings and Conclusions

A brief summary of the study stating the problem, the objective, the methodology and the major findings is presented in this chapter. This implication of the study is then discussed, suggesting a few areas for further research.

STATEMENT OF THE PROBLEMS

The problem is titled as CREATIVITY AND SOCIAL MATURITY OF TEACHER TRAINEES.

OBJECTIVES OF THE STUDY

The following were the objectives of the study.

1. To find out the significance of difference in the fluency level of men and women teacher trainees.
2. To find out the significance of difference in the flexibility level of men and women teacher trainees.
3. To find out the significance of difference in the originality level of men of women teacher trainees.
4. To find out the significance of difference in the personal adequacy of men of women teacher trainees.
5. To find out the significance of difference in the interpersonal adequacy of men of women teacher trainees.

6. To find out the significance of difference in the social adequacy of men of women teacher trainees.
7. To find out the significance of difference in the social maturity of men of women teacher trainees.
8. To find out the significance of difference between teacher trainees studying in Government and Government aided institutions with respect to fluency level.
9. To find out the significance of difference between teacher trainees studying in Government and Government aided institutions with respect to flexibility level.
10. To find out the significance of difference between teacher trainees studying in Government and Government aided institutions with respect to originality level.
11. To find out the significance of difference between teacher trainees studying in Government and Government Aided institutions with respect to personal adequacy in social maturity.
12. To find out the significance of difference between teacher trainees studying in Government and Government Aided institutions with respect to Interpersonal adequacy in social maturity.
13. To find out the significance of difference between teacher trainees studying in Government and Government Aided institutions with respect to social adequacy in social maturity.
14. To find out the significance of difference between teacher trainees studying in Government and Government Aided institutions with respect to overall social maturity.
15. To find out the significance of difference between teacher trainees studying in Government and Government Aided institutions with respect to fluency level in creativity.
16. To find out the significance of difference between teacher trainees studying in first year and second year with respect to flexibility level in creativity.
17. To find out the significance of difference between teacher trainees studying in first year and second year with respect to originality level in creativity.
18. To find out the significance of difference between teacher trainees studying in first year and second year with respect to personal adequacy in the social maturity scale.
19. To find out the significance of difference between teacher trainees studying in first year and second year with respect to interpersonal adequacy in the social maturity scale.

20. To find out the significance of difference between teacher trainees studying in first year and second year with respect to social adequacy in the social maturity scale.
21. To find out the significance of difference between teacher trainees studying in first year and second year with respect to overall social maturity.
22. To find out the significance of difference between the teacher trainees in the creativity factors based on their father's qualifications.
23. To find out the significance of difference between the teacher trainees in social maturity based on their father's qualifications.
24. To find out the significance of difference between the teacher trainees in the creativity factors based on their mother's qualifications.
25. To find out the significance of difference between the teacher trainees in the social maturity based on their mother's qualifications.
26. To find out the significance of difference between the teacher trainees in the creativity factors based on their parental income.
27. To find out the significance of difference between the teacher trainees in the social maturity based on their parental income.
28. To find out the relationship between creativity dimensions and personal adequacy of teacher trainees.
29. To find out the relationship between creativity dimensions and interpersonal adequacy of teacher trainees.
30. To find out the relationship between creativity dimensions and social adequacy of teacher trainees.
31. To find out the relationship between creativity dimensions and social maturity of teacher trainees.

HYPOTHESES OF THE STUDY

1. There is a significant difference in the fluency level between men and women teacher trainees.
2. There is a significant difference in the flexibility level between men and women teacher trainees.
3. There is a significant difference in the originality level between men and women teacher trainees.
4. There is a significant difference in the personal adequacy between men and women teacher trainees.
5. There is a significant difference in the interpersonal between men and women teacher trainees.
6. There is a significant difference in the social adequacy between men and women teacher trainees.

7. There is a significant difference in the social maturity between men and women teacher trainees.
8. There is a significant difference between teacher trainees studying in Government and Aided Institutions with respect to fluency level.
9. There is a significant difference between teacher trainees studying in Government and Aided Institutions with respect to flexibility level.
10. There is a significant difference between teacher trainees studying in Government and Aided Institutions with respect to originality level.
11. There is a significant difference between teacher trainees studying in Government and Aided Institutions with respect to personal adequacy on social maturity.
12. There is a significant difference between teacher trainees studying in Government and Aided Institutions with respect to Interpersonal adequacy on social maturity.
13. There is a significant difference between teacher trainees studying in Government and Aided Institutions with respect to social adequacy on social maturity.
14. There is a significant difference between teacher trainees studying in Government and Aided Institutions with respect to social maturity.
15. There is a significant difference between teacher trainees studying in first year and second year with respect to fluency level on creativity.
16. There is a significant difference between teacher trainees studying in first year and second year with respect to flexibility level on creativity.
17. There is a significant difference between teacher trainees studying in first year and second year with respect to originality level on creativity.
18. There is a significant difference between teacher trainees studying in first year and second year with respect to personal adequacy on social maturity scale.
19. There is a significant difference between teacher trainees studying in first year and second year with respect to interpersonal adequacy on social maturity scale.
20. There is a significant difference between teacher trainees studying in first year and second year with respect to Social adequacy on social maturity scale.
21. There is a significant difference between teacher trainees studying in first year and second year with respect to social maturity scale.
22. There is a significant difference between teacher trainees of the creativity factors based on their father's qualifications.
23. There is a significant difference between teacher trainees of the social maturity based on their father's qualifications.

24. There is a significant difference between teacher trainees of the creativity factors based on their mother's qualifications.
25. There is a significant difference between teacher trainees of the social maturity based on their mother's qualifications.
26. There is a significant difference between teacher trainees of the creativity factors based on their parental income.
27. There is a significant difference between teacher trainees of the social maturity based on their father's qualifications.
28. There is significant relationship between creativity dimensions and personal adequacy of teacher trainees.
29. There is significant relationship between creativity dimensions and interpersonal adequacy of teacher trainees.
30. There is significant relationship between creativity dimensions and social adequacy of teacher trainees.
31. There is significant relationship between creativity dimensions and social maturity of teacher trainees.

TOOLS USED IN THIS STUDY

In order to verify the hypotheses the following tools have been used.

- Creativity test by Baquer Mehid
- Rao's Social Maturity Scale.

The Sampling technique used was Staffed Random Sampling. The study was conducted among 225 secondary grade teacher trainees drawn from different Training Institutes.

MAJOR FINDINGS

1. The mean scores obtained for the men and women teacher trainees for fluency level of creativity shows those female members scores higher than the male teacher trainees.
2. The mean scores obtained for the men and women teacher trainees for flexibility level of creativity shows those female members scores higher than the male teacher trainees and it is statistically proved and thus the hypothesis is retained.
3. It was found that a significant difference occurred in the originality of men and women teacher trainees.
4. The mean scores obtained for the men and women teacher trainees for personal adequacy of social maturity shows that women teacher trainees are having more personal adequacy than the men teacher trainees.
5. For the interpersonal adequacy of social maturity showed that male members scores higher than the female teacher trainees.

6. It was found that there was no significant difference in the social adequacy of men and women teacher trainees.
7. There was no significant difference in the social maturity of men and women teacher trainees.
8. It was found that there was no significant difference in the fluency and originality level of teacher trainees studying in Government and Government Aided Institutes. In the case of flexibility level significant difference was found among the teacher trainees.
9. Significant differences were found between teacher trainees studying Government and Government Aided Secondary Grade Training Institutes on their social adequacy, personal adequacy, interpersonal and social maturity.
10. It was found that there was no significant difference in the flexibility and originality level of teacher trainees studying first year and second year teacher trainees. In the case of fluency level significant difference was found among the teacher trainees.
11. In the case of social maturity and its dimensions significant differences were not found between the teacher trainees studying first year and second year courses.
12. Parental qualifications, income of the parents, and their educational qualifications have no significant influence on the creativity and social maturity of the teacher trainees.

EDUCATIONAL IMPLICATIONS

One of the objectives of carrying out this research is to arrive at specific conclusions. Conclusions are essentially an important outcome of research and are derived from the data analysis and interpretations. The aim of the present study was to study creativity and social maturity of secondary grade teacher trainees.

When analyzing creativity is, it is helpful to consider creativity as something that is necessary for the discovery of creative solutions to problems. Solving problems is not just a scientific or engineering activity; even educationists are commissioned to express a concept or an idea in a certain way.

Following the theme of creative solutions to problems, what makes one solution creative and another simply ordinary. It seems that it is often to context within which solution is offered that establishes creativity. This means that creativity is not simple simply a mental process there may be little to distinguish creativity from expertise. Creative solutions are very much need for the problem active society. It is very essential for the teacher trainees to train them to have a creative solution in the classrooms. So social maturity is very much needed for the teacher trainees also.

In this study it was found that the teacher trainees are not much different in their social maturity as well as their creativity level based on their gender, type of management of the institutions and their year of study also. Parental qualifications and parental income may not show significant influence on the creativity dimensions and social maturity and its dimensions. The teacher training institutions make a significant role in including the creativity and social maturity the teacher trainees.

The institutions should chalks out programmes to nourish creativity among the teacher trainees. The flexible curriculum the democratic administration through councils an committees, scientific and recreational hobbies, dramatics, writing competitions painting debates, cultural activities not only develop their creativity but also make them to be a well matured person. The trainees become a good creative teacher. A creative teacher is sensitive to the problems arising either in the classrooms or in the school and has got the capacity to suggest more than one solution to solve these problems.

SUGGESTIONS FOR FURTHER RESEARCH

This study does not confine itself to the survey of secondary grade teacher trainees in the Chennai Educational district only and therefore cannot claim to have comprehensiveness nor can its conclusions be claimed to be universally valid. This is however a beginning and the results hold promise to lead a more comprehensive and in depth investigation into the interaction between creativity and social maturity.

For more universal and unbiased results, this study may be replicated with the following modifications.

1. Relationship between the creativity and learning styles of the teacher trainees can be undertaken.
2. Relationship between creativity, Hemisphericity and achievement motivation can be analysed.
3. Relationship between creativity, social intelligence and personality types can be studied.

❒

16

Climate and Job Satisfaction of Teachers

Teachers are the backbone of the educational process and play a vital role in building the nation. Teachers act as a pivot around which all the educational programmes rotate and they are crucial in the implementation process also. It is also a fact that the quality of teachers influences the level of achievement of students. Teachers have an impact on all the desired outcomes envisaged in an individual by the society. Thus the role of teachers does not limit itself to impart the knowledge alone, but in broadening the national outlook, enhancing sense of efficacy and competency among the future citizens and preparing individuals for the right type of profession.

CONCEPT OF A PROFESSION

A profession has certain level of skill and knowledge before put to practice. Entry to the profession is thus restricted to those who have already acquired the requisite skills and knowledge. All members of a profession are expected to have a minimum level of competence and share a general belief in what counts good practice.

Professionals have good specific sense of purpose and responsibility and they are bound by codes of ethics that outline how they operate in their professional life. Professionals are generally respected because they have skills that are valuable to the society.

TEACHING AS A PROFESSION

Teaching qualifies the fundamentals of a profession and it posses the qualities of sincere devotion for the betterment of human (Wise 1994) Human interaction gives personal touch in the educational process and that takes place in school environment plays an important role in shaping students in the classroom. "The destiny of India is being shaped in the class room" and - teachers influence the behaviour of students as per Kothari Commission Report on Education 1964-66. Hence, school is a place where web of interaction takes place together among varied people including teacher's students and organizational people creates interactive environment leads to an organizational climate.

Job satisfaction is important to the employee, the worker and the community. The community profits on the score of an individual and well being of the society in general the understanding of the dynamics of job satisfaction therefore requires serious consideration of all concerned. Teaching is one of the most common professions in the society. Job satisfaction among teachers is one of the problems that the administration faces. When the teacher engages in a plan to achieve higher school effectiveness the performance and effectiveness of the teacher and school also improves. For improving job satisfaction among teachers, environment of the institution should be such in which teacher obtain social need satisfaction and enjoy a sense of accomplishment in their job.

THE CONCEPT OF JOB SATISFACTION

Job satisfaction is concerned with the feelings one has toward the job. The satisfaction one gets from out of tasks assigned to him in his job. People especially those above the lower rung of an organization feel adequately rewarded only when the jobs are challenging and help to exploit their latent talents to the maximum.

Job satisfaction as a "reintegration of effect produced by individual perception of fulfillment of his needs in relation to his work and the situations surrounding it. In the other hand job satisfaction refers to a general attitude towards work by an individual worker"(Syadain 1995).

DEFINITION OF JOB SATISFACTION

Job satisfaction may be viewed as the pleasurable emotional state resulting from the perceptions of one's job as fulfilling or allowing the fulfillment of one's needs, Edwin A Locke,(1976). According to P.C.Smith (1990) job satisfaction is the persistent feeling towards different aspects of the job situation. E.A. Locke (1969) admits the job satisfaction and job dissatisfaction are seen as function of perceived relationship between the one wants from are job and what are perceived it as offering or entailing. Job satisfaction may be global or specific. Sometimes job satisfaction is referred to as overall feeling of satisfaction (i.e. Global satisfaction). At some other point of times job satisfaction refers to person's feeling towards specific dimensions of the work.

DETERMINANTS OF JOB SATISFACTION

Many factors influence job satisfaction of employees. Review of research reveals the following important determinants of job satisfaction.

1. **Supervision:** The first and foremost important determinants of job satisfaction are supervision and the style of leadership.
2. **Job Content:** Another influential factor of job satisfaction is the job content. Job content refers to the factors such as recognition, responsibility, advancement, achievement etc. in the jobs employee perform.
3. **Specialization:** The relationship between job specialization and job satisfaction is complex and that leads to greater efficiency in general, but at the some time it lowers the job satisfaction to some people with increasing but after a particular point it starts falling. That is to say after a certain point specialization, it leads to dissatisfaction.
4. **Educational level:** Keeping the occupational level as constant there is found a negative correlation between the level of education of employees and their satisfaction. A Possible explanation could be that people with educated level have a tendency to set higher expectation from their jobs. Dissatisfaction will be more when an educated person is employed in lower grades.
5. **Age:** The relationship between age and job satisfaction is both complex and fascinating. Research reveals that old workers are satisfied workers. Job satisfaction usually tends to be high when people enter the work force.
6. **Race and Sex:** Sex and race also affects job satisfaction. It has been found that job satisfaction among blacks and other minority groups has been consistently lower that that of whites in America. When males and females were equally affected by such determinants of job satisfaction as wages, prestige and supervisory positions.

CONSEQUENCES OF JOB DISSATISFACTION

Job dissatisfaction can act as a double-edged sword as it reduced absenteeism and labour turn over.

Absenteeism

There exist a relationship between the job satisfaction and frequency of absence of employees weather unexcused absence due to minor ailments. Absenteeism is inversely related to the level of job satisfaction.

Turnover

Research has clearly established that the satisfied worker is less likely than his dissatisfied counterpart to quit the job overtime.

Negative publicity

Another frequently notable consequence of job dissatisfaction is badmouthing the organization. That is disgruntled emplo0yee verbalizes his discontent.

THE CONCETPT OF ORGANIZATIONAL CLIMATE

In 1950's and 1960's a new line of enquiry captured the attention of the researchers in the field of natural and social sciences. This line of enquiry introduced the concept of environment and organizational climate in to the field of educational research. Studies of 'environments' of organizations became quick popular with the social scientists, particularly with those who are interested in the studies of organizations, their characteristics and effectiveness. After 1970 a new emphasis was laid on the study of human environment. A movement was started to make an all out effort to upgrade the quality of human life. This created a strong concern for improving the social environment of the human milieu. Hence studies of organizational environment have quite often focused on organizational climate also. In fact scientists have used different methods and dimensions for characterizing organizational environments. Thus a distinction that is drawn between the organizational environment and organizational climate is that of 'part' and the 'whole' organizational climate constitutes a specific dimension of the total environment, which may be defined as the environment of an organization.

DEFINITIONS OF ORGANIZATIONAL CLIMATE

It has been classified on the basis of the existing literature that organizational climate is an aspect of organization's total environment, a characteristics that give a unique quality to the environment. Hence quite often the term 'environment' has been used in place of 'climate'. Physiological environment is considered more often an identical form for 'organizational climate'. Thus number of terms such as atmosphere, climate, physiological environment, ethos, social interaction, inter personal relationships, social emotional climate etc., have been used in literature interchangeably. Benjamin Bloom(1978) regards organizational climate as " a network of forces and factors which surround engulf and play on the individual. The environment is a shaping and reinforcing force which acts on the individuals". Miskel(1987) defines climate with special reference to inter personal relations of people in the organization. He calls this "interpersonal climate" and describes it as the behaviour, attitude and perceptions of the individuals within the building as they interact with each other. Hellreigel and slocum (1984) pointed out that an effective climate is a simple and static environment may prove to be dysfunctional in a dynamic and complex environment. At the same time it should be noted that the climates of different organizational subsystems are seldom radically different. Therefore, instead of taking a fragmented view of climate in a particular sub-system the total system may be more meaningful to study and analyse.

The school is a people developing or changing socio, psychological organization. The interaction of organizational behaviour within the school gives rise to the climate or personality of the school. Better teaching and learning depends on the climate of schools. Organizational climate is a global construct and creates a common phenomenon in reading various climates of organization viz. learning environment academic climate, social climate, learning climate etc.,

School organizational climate is always measure in terms of healthy interpersonal dynamics. All human organizations have certain essential features. Firstly they have an objective of a good result to be achieved. Secondly there is structure, the way that people are placed in working relationship with each other. Research shows that school climate can affect many areas and people with in schools. For example a positive climate has been associated with fewer behavioural and emotional problems for students. (Kuperminc et al., 2001)

School climate is multi-dimensional and influenced by many factors including students, parents, teachers, management (School personnel) and the community. Additionally school climate can siginificantly impact the educational environment as Freibeg(1998) notes "School climate can be a positive influence on health of learning environment or a significant barrier to learning.

FACTORS AFFECTING ORGANIZATIONAL CLIMATE

In every organization there exist certain elements that exert profound influence on the existing climate. In some organizations certain factors like structures and process play major role, where as in others the level of Technology may be the major influential factor in climate. Lawrence James and Allen Jones (1974) have tried to identify the factors influencing climate and they grouped these factors under 5 heads.

- Organizational content
- Organizational structure
- Process
- Physical environment
- System values and norms

TYPOLOGY OF CLIMATE

Halpin and croft identified that there are six organizational climates

1. **The open Climate:** The open climate teachers enjoy extremely high esprit and they work well together. They are not overloaded and they have job satisfaction. The principal works hard to set an example to the teachers. He criticizes the actions of the teachers whenever necessary. He considers the social needs of the teachers and helps them. He is in full control of the situation and he clearly provides leadership among teachers
2. **The Autonomous Climate:** The teachers enjoy almost complete freedom in the autonomous climate. They are satisfied with their job and work well together. The principal has set up procedures and regulations to facilitate the teacher's task. The teachers are allowed to do things analytically and creatively.
3. **The Controlled Climate:** Every teacher works hard under the controlled climate with emphasis on the task. It is task oriented and not employee centered. Teachers are not allowed to do work as they like and the heads controls them. The principal allows little flexibility.
4. **The Familiar Climate:** Here the relationship between the teacher and the principal is friendly in manner. Social need satisfaction is extremely high. The principal exerts little control in directing their activities. The principal helps teachers freely and exercises leadership in an indirect manner and tries to keep production satisfactory. The principal's behaviour is job oriented but does not hinder the social needs satisfaction on the part of the teachers.

The Paternal Climate

Under the paternal climate the teachers do not work well together. They are split into fractions. The headmaster's attempt is ineffective to control the teachers and there is only a very little hope to satisfy their social needs. The faculty has to work in the way the principal wants but at the same time the principal as the paternal guardian of the school faculty does not ignore the individual interest and hence his behaviour is perceived as highly considerate (Sharma 1973, p.264)

Closed Climate

The teachers are dissatisfied with respect to the task achievement or social needs in schools where the closed climate prevails. It is not a genuine climate and it is characterized by a high degree of apathy on the part of all members of organization. The organization is not moving. This climate lacks authenticity of behaviour. The principal constrains the emergence of leadership acts from the group. The group members secure neither social needs satisfaction nor job satisfaction stemming from task-accomplishment (Sharma 1973,p.266).

Additionally specific research on school climate in high-risk urban environments indicated that a positive supportive and culturally conscious school climate could significantly shape the degree of academic success experienced by urban students (Haynes &Comer 1993).

The job satisfaction of teachers is important for any educational institutions and it is not new to educational thinking

STATEMENT OF THE PROBLEM

The problem under investigation is Organizational Climate and Job Satisfaction of Higher Secondary School Teachers.

DEFINITION OF TECHNICAL TERMS USED IN THE STUDY

- **Organizational Climate:** In the present study the organizational climate refers to administrative and behavioural aspects of heads of schools
- **Job Satisfaction:** Job satisfaction refers to teachers happiness over facilities, security, working condition and liking for the job.

NEED AND SIGNIFICANCE OF THE STUDY

Many researches were conducted to find out the relationship between organizational climate and job satisfaction among college teachers. The research findings on this topic are concentrated mostly on discovering rather than creating a climate although investigators have envisaged the eventful possibility of selecting climate for maximum benefit. Hence this is certainly an area, which needs to be investigated. At the same time, the establishment of an appropriate climate also becomes one of the functions of administrations. The results of the study could bring out the prevailing condition of organizational climate and job satisfaction among higher secondary teachers of Madurai and suggestions could be made for a better organizational set up, consequently a better work morale.

OBJECTIVES OF STUDY

1. To study the organizational climate of schools under different types of management
2. To study the level of job satisfaction of higher secondary school teachers.
3. To study the level of job satisfaction with respect to gender.
4. To find out the significant difference between the job satisfaction of higher secondary teachers with respect to their length of experience
5. To find out the significant difference between the job satisfaction of higher secondary teachers with respect to the type of school.
6. To find out the significant difference between the job satisfaction of higher secondary school teachers with respect to their locality of the school.
7. To find out the significant difference between the job satisfaction of higher secondary teachers with respect to their monthly income.
8. To find out the correlation between the job satisfaction of higher secondary school with respect to their monthly income.
9. To study the level of job satisfaction of higher secondary school teachers under different types of management
10. To find out the interrelationship between organizational climate and job satisfaction of higher secondary school teachers.

❐

17

Review of Literature

This chapter aims in presenting background materials for the development of the present Investigation and also provided the investigator with rich and varied information in the fundamentals of the present problem. A summary of the writings of the recognized authors and the previous research provides evidence that the investigator can move from what is already known to what is still unknown. Review makes the investigator to be interested in knowing the achievements of researchers and helps to understand the significance of the discoveries. Since the effective research is based upon the past knowledge this step is also helpful to eliminate the duplication of the work. It has given the investigator a sound knowledge of all aspects of the problem chosen as a whole, helps to sharpen and define understanding of the existing knowledge in the problem area and also suggested the possible techniques and procedures to be assumed and applied in the current study.

RELATED STUDIES ON ORGANIZATIONAL CLIMATE

A large proportion of studies surveyed the existing organizational climate of schools, colleges and universities.

Baylay (1957), Pace, Stern (1970) and others view environment as a powerful determinant of behaviour. **Sharma (1969) Sharma,Buch and Rai(1971) Mubayi** and **Sharma(1971)** found that schools differ in terms of their climates(environment). **Sharma (1971)** found that students academic performance has significant relationship with school climate. **Sharma and Santhanam (1971 and 1972)** studied relationship of school climate with classroom teacher behaviour. Sharma and **Quraishi (1972)** explored in to relationship between school climate and teachers morale. Sharma and **Quraishi (1972)** explored in to relationship between school climate and teachers morale. **Sharma (1973)** and Sharma and Parham (1973) studied the relationship between, school climate and initiating the structure behaviour and consideration behaviour of school heads respectively. **Sharma (1972)** studied school climate in relation with leadership behaviour of the headmaster. **Sharma (1975)** also studied the relationship of school climate with school effectiveness and teacher satisfaction along with other variables. **Sharma (1974)** found headmaster's effectiveness as significant predictor of school climate. **Sharma (1973)** conducted replication study along the lines of its originators and found new dimensions of climate and developed model profiles for Indian schools which have been discussed in this technical Manual. The book "Diagnosing the school climate" by **Sharma (1978)** gives, details about the development of the school organizational climate questionnaire. Studies referred above have indicated that school climate is related with student performance, teachers satisfaction school and headmaster effectiveness, leadership behaviour of the headmaster and many such other variables. All results have indicated that school environment warrants our immediate attention.

The dimensions of mostly touched upon over intellectual (anality of teaching, research, academic freedom etc., social moral trust, cohesiveness, communication, support, interpersonal relations) and administrative communication, disciplinary policy and structure. Differences were observed between the climate perceptions of faculty and administrators **(Anderson 1983)** the anti-creativity climate was reported in most of the institutions **(Jex 1983,Gibb1968, Ellison et al., 1968,Taylor1982)** the capacity for innovation was facilitated by openness of climate and by teacher morale as well **(Pillai, 1979)**

The above picture of overall organizational climates of Educational Institutions was not quite clear on the other end of the climate and formed a normal distribution. The largest number came into the intermediate range high on some attitudes and low on others.

A number of studies linked the climate of institutions to the size of the institutions in forms of faculty and students. The size of an institution was found to have a mixed effect on climate, positive for some aspects and negative on others. **(Duttlinger 1979,Bhatnagar 1979,China – Tangual, 1980)** Negative association between these two was pointed by **Rickout 1975 and shelt 1979.But Kumar1979, Metha 1979** and **Birch 1982** found them all to be independent of each other.

These studies on educational administration reported its functions and pressure on it, which found a strong relationship, exist between macro social work activities and climate. **May Carolyn Stdwey 1984** use activities index (AI) and (OCI) organizational climate index in evaluation and comparing climate in school organization. The activity index discriminated between groups as expected.

Teachers' perception of school climate may be influenced by additional factors besides the principals leadership behaviours reported by **scott and John Erren Jr on 1998.**

RELATED STUDIES ON ORGANIZATIONAL CLIMATE AND FACULTY MORALE

A substantial part of the studies under this category explored relationship of teacher morale with organizational climate. Halpin and Croft initiated this trend. They found faculty morale to be one of the important dimensions of school climate. Faculty morale was found closely tied to organizational climate **(Sharma and Quaraishi, 1972;Murphy 1975; Aderunumu and Chinatangual, 1980)**

Studies in **1979** by **Pillai,Collica and Mehore** found faculty morale to be positively associated with organizational climate (Openness,achievement,leadership behaviour) Institutions with open climate were found to be higher on ;the ladder of morale as compared to other groups.

RELATED STUDIES ON ORGANIZATIONAL CLIMATE AND STUDENT PERFORMANCE

Studies suggested that climates high in control were not conductive to the establishment of moral climate but led to behavioural problems of students. Aspects of social control like production emphasis disengagement hindrance etc affected all participants in an organization (**Plimpton 1979; Raburn 1979**).

Students and teachers differed in their attitudes to climate conditions and positive attitudes were tied to better climate (**Rao 1971**and **Friedmann 1979**).

Studies indicated that a given climate condition may result in specific attitudes and behavioral responses by teachers and students and that one may affect the other.

STUDIES RELATED ON JOB SATISFACTION

Foreign studies related to Job satisfaction

Marlow (1996) studied the attitude of teachers through survey method and the study found that 44 percent of the teachers occasionally considered leaving the profession. Reason cited included student discipline, students' lack of motivation and poor attitudes, emotional factors such as lack of fulfillment boredom with the daily routine stress and frustration, lack of respect from the community, parents, administrators, and/ or students, difficult working condition, and low salaries. Also 49 percent of the population surveyed identified the professional prestige to be as they had expected it or better.

Lam peter (1995) studied 350 teacher trainees of Singapore's teacher training institution in their relationship among quality of work life carrier commitment, job satisfaction and withdrawal cognition. Carrier commitment perceptions of the social status of teaching strongly related to commitment to and satisfaction with teaching.

Clarke Robert (1995) found out the teachers job satisfaction instrument by brainstorming session with 81 teachers in Pennsylvania and the results were converted in to numerical scores and the findings revealed that pay did not appear to be a satisfier or dissatisfier, that interaction with students was the most satisfying factor and that majority of the subjects should approve of their children following in their factor and teachers were not happy with the state mandated innovations of outcome based education(OBE) and inclusion(NAV)

Kim I (1994) investigated predictors of teacher job satisfaction as these predictors through the sample of 2,054 practicing class room teachers. Through their findings the teachers job satisfaction are associated with both intrinsic and extrinsic rewards. That is, the factors salary and opportunities for advancement are generally perceived as extrinsic sources of satisfaction. Job satisfaction such as profession challenge, professional autonomy working conditions interaction with colleagues and interaction with students are generally classified as intrinsic satisfiers. Intrinsic satisfiers refer to factors that make certain activities rewar4ding in themselves. This study has potential of maximizing the achievement of organizational and individual goals through improvement of teacher job satisfaction.

Saad IA (1996) studied the job satisfaction in transitional society with in some of the Arabian schools and found that the satisfaction of teachers relies with work itself and with social needs too. Also finds that female teachers and teachers with higher educational levels were more likely to be satisfied with their jobs.

Heller H studied the relationship between teacher job satisfaction and principal leadership style.

Here about 45% of the 339 teachers were queried and found dissatisfied. The teachers were least satisfied with teachings financial aspects and most satisfied with co- workers. Job satisfaction was not significantly related to principal leadership style

A survey was conducted by **Hoppock(1935)** on teachers job satisfaction. The sample of this study was five hundred teachers from North Eastern United

States. The job satisfaction was estimated through four attitude scales. By combining these scales a measure of job satisfaction was obtained. Among the sample the most satisfied hundred and the least satisfied hundred was compared and the satisfied were differentiated from the dissatisfied teachers. The satisfied showed fewer indications of maladjustments and enjoyed better human relationships with their superiors. They were more religious and had selected their vocations on their own. They had seven and half years of experience in teaching. The main causes of dissatisfaction were monotony and fatigue.

Anjaneyulu(1968) conducted a study of job satisfaction among secondary school teachers and its impact on the education of pupils with special reference to the state of Andhra Pradesh. This study sought to find out the reasons for dissatisfaction among teachers working under different conditions. A sample of 1000 teachers was taken up using stratified random sampling technique in the Andra Pradesh State. The main findings were that factors like frequent transfers, low standard of teachers caused dissatisfaction among teachers. Indiscipline among pupils, lack of parental cooperation, lack of bright prospects in the job, lack of job security, rigid and orthodox service conditions and too much dominations by the management were found to be the chief factors of dissatisfaction.

The job satisfaction of teachers in secondary school depends on the economic and social status and the poor such conditions causing dissatisfaction among teachers in secondary school was reported by **Anjaneyulu 1973.** Rigid rules orthodox service conditions and lack of parental cooperation are the causes of dissatisfaction among teachers working in government institutions.

Sing H L (1974) and **Goyal J.C (1980)** and **Thakkar P.A (1977)** suggested that there was a significant relationship between teachers attitudes and job satisfaction.

Kulsum N (1995) correlated a relationship between the dependent and independent variables. Teachers working in corporation schools were highly satisfied than those who were working in other types of schools. Amarsigh(1985)) correlated job satisfaction among different professionals for teachers engineers, advocates and doctors.

RELATED STUDIES ON ORGANISATIONAL CLIMATE AND JOB SATISFACTION

Most of the studies on organizational climate are based on organizational climate descriptive questionnaire. The studies included here reveal that the majority of the Indian schools have a closed climate followed by open and autonomous climates **(Baraiya 1985,Swatandra Devi 1985** and **Prakasham, 1986)** Most of these studies related to organizational climate with set of other variable like teacher morale, job satisfaction performance of the students etc. Class room climate found to play a crucial role in student achievement **(Uma Devi 1983;Lalithakumari 1984; singles 1984;** and **santhappan 1984)** Disengagement among teachers was found to be related negatively to school effectiveness while feeling of esprit and feeling of intimacy were found related to school effectiveness (**Srivastava 1985,Sriratna 1983)**. The promotions of a favourable organizational climate for creativity helped to increase productivity, satisfaction and mental health of workers **(Ganesan 1987)**

Organizational climates viz esprit, trust, consideration and total leadership behaviour are correlated with job satisfaction **(Balvender** and **Kaur 1986)** Student activism had a relationship of heads, teachers and improper methods of teaching **(Rama 1978,Bassano, Louis V 1997)** indicated that climate membership was significantly related to job satisfaction and performance. **Pparaji and Timoty I 1988** suggested that teacher were dissatisfied with their jobs and perceived the school system as being unhealthy it suggest that administrators could enhance job satisfaction in their school by improving organizational climate.

Greaves 1991 reported that there is a direct positive correlation between school scoring on the openness index and job satisfaction. **Alltrunian and Anita Rose 1992** decided that teachers working within the inter-disciplinary middle school perceived a greater degree of job satisfaction and perceived their school climate. The teachers perceived inter-disciplinary schools as having more open climate with high thrust, esprit engagement and satisfaction than did departmentalized schools.

Dimkpa P (1992) studied the impact of organizational climate and job satisfaction on black and white managerial job satisfaction. One hindered and twenty-four managers were assessed on their satisfaction level. Results indicated that black managerial job satisfaction and organizational climate significantly differs from each other and significantly influence one another. Results also suggest that retail organizations may not ready themselves for the multi-racial workforce of the future.

MillerB (1990) studied the job satisfaction among the Indian vocational home economics teachers.

Job satisfaction measured by the bray field index of job satisfaction and was found to be low. As per the result as the participation increase the job satisfaction decreased. Analysis of variance indicated a significant difference in job satisfaction between teachers who participated in eight or more activities and those who did not.

Craig FM (1992) has done a survey of organizational climate on the institutional research memo to all the faculty members and administrators at three campuses of the mid plains community college area. The survey instrument utilized likert scale to examine seven areas of institutional functioning and work environments. Study findings were compared to 1989 national norms for faculty and administrator attitudes. Study highlights included the following: (1) of the seven areas examined in the survey, there was least satisfaction among all groups in the area of rewards (relating to salary, benefits and personal growth), 64.8 %of the faculty and 52.9% of administrators rated work conditions as satisfactory or very satisfactory as compared with 63.5% and 74% for the national norms, respectively.

CONCLUSION

Based on the above review, the suitable methodology and procedure for the present investigation are given in detailed in the following chapter.

❐

18

Research Design and Method

This chapter explains about the hypotheses relating to job satisfaction and organizational climate of higher secondary school teachers. The teachers of higher secondary schools have been classified on the basis of their respective managements viz Aided, Government and private.

Influence of sociological factors like gender length of experience locale salary on job satisfaction of higher secondary school teachers were also considered.

The present investigation is a survey type of research. The main objective of the present investigation is to find out whether a significant relationship exists between the organizational climate and job satisfaction of high school teachers and to find out the influence of background variables such as gender, type of management, experience, salary etc.

The following hypotheses were formulated based on the objectives framed and cited in the first chapter.

HYPOTHESES

1. There will be a significant difference in the organizational climate of schools under different types of management.
2. There will be a significant difference in the organizational climate of aided and government higher secondary teachers.
3. There will be a significant difference in the organizational climate of aided and private higher secondary school teachers.

4. There will be a significant difference in the organizational climate of government and private higher secondary teachers.
5. The over all job satisfaction of higher secondary schoolteachers will be high.
6. The gender difference has a hindrance on the level of job satisfaction of higher secondary school teachers with respect to their length of experience
7. There will be a significant difference in the level of job satisfaction of higher secondary school teachers with respect to their length of experience
8. There will be a significant difference in the level of job satisfaction of higher secondary school teachers under different types of management
9. There will be a significant difference in the level of job satisfaction of higher secondary teachers in aided and government schools
10. There will be a significant difference in the level of job satisfaction of higher secondary teachers in aided and private schools.
11. There will be a significant difference in the level of job satisfaction of higher secondary teachers in private and government schools.
12. There will be a significant positive correlation between organizational climate and job satisfaction of higher secondary school teachers.

RESEARCH TOOLS USED

- Tool 1: School Organizational Climate Description Questionnaire (SOCDQ) developed by Sharma M (1978)
- Tool 2: Teachers Job Satisfaction Scale (TJSS) developed by Mudgil Y (1998)

ORGANIZATIONAL CLIMATE DESCRIPTIVE QUESTIONNAIRE

Description

The organizational climate descriptive questionnaire was meant to collect information from high school teachers. It consists of 63 items of which first 32 items were meant for assessing teacher behaviours and remaining 31 items were to rate the administrative behaviour of the heads of the schools. The distribution of the number of items to assess teachers behaviour is as follows.

DISTRIBUTION OF ITEMS UNDER DIFFERENT SUBTESTS

S.No.	Sub Tests Perceived Behavioural Aspects of Teachers	Items
1.	Disengagement	1,8,21,32,36,44,52,55,57
2.	Alienation	18,30,39,50
3.	Espirit	3,11,17,24,33,38,45,53,58

S.No.	Sub Tests Perceived Behavioural Aspects of Teachers	Items
4.	Intimacy	5,12,25,34,40,46,54,60
5.	Psychophsical Hindrance	9,23,26,41,47,63
6.	Controls	15,20,27,42,48,63
7.	Production Emphasis	6,14,28,35,43,48,64
8.	Humanized Thrust	2,4,7,10,13,16,19,22,29,31,37,51,56,59

JOB SATISFACTION SCALE

Description

Job satisfaction tool was administered to study the job satisfaction of higher secondary school teachers. It considered 60 items.

ADMINISTRATION

The test was administered personally to higher secondary school teachers who were required to put a tick mark in the appropriate column against the statements indicating the extent of job satisfaction on a five point scale as 1) Strongly agree 2) Agree 3) Undecided 4) Disagree 5) Strongly Disagree

SCORING

Evolving a tentative scheme of weight age quantitatively treats the response to the job satisfaction test.

In each dimension there are questions with positive and negative attitudes. The score for the response on the 5-point scale and the questions with positive attitudes were scored as follows.

1.	Strongly agree	5
2.	Agree	4
3.	Undecided	3
4.	Disagree	2
5.	Strongly Disagree	1

The score for the response for the response on the 5-point scale questions with negative attitudes were scored in a reverse order as mentioned above. The maximum no of items with positive attitude is 32 and negative attitude is 28.

SAMPLE

For the present study various higher secondary schools located at Madurai district was selected. Twelve Schools were randomly chosen for investigation and questionnaires were administered to the all the postgraduate assistants. Among them, 100 from aided school, 100 from Government school and 100 from private schools. Out of 300 150 respondents were males and 150 were females.

TABLE. 18.1: Distribution of Sample

Sl.No	Type of School	Frequency	Percentage
1.	Government	62	22.71
2.	Aided	108	39.56
3.	Private	103	37.73

TABLE. 18.2: Distribution of Sample with Respect to Gender

Sl No	Type of School	No of Males	No of Females	Total
1	Government	25	37	62
2	Aided	56	52	108
3	Private	37	66	103
	Total	**118**	**155**	**273**

TABLE. 18.3: Distribution of Sample with Respect to Locality

Sl.No	Type of School	Locality		
		Rural	Urban	Total
1.	Government	31	31	62
2.	Aided	70	39	109
3.	Matriculation	15	87	102
	Total	116	157	273

MAIN STUDY

The main study deals with the procedure followed in administering the tests and in collecting data. The samples were randomly chosen from the higher secondary school. The samples of the higher secondary school teachers thus selected wee tested for variables of the present study using organizational climate descriptive questionnaire and job satisfaction test, which have been workable in the pilot study.

The following statistical measures were used in the present study to analyse and interpret the data.

Formula for finding standard deviation (S.D)

I = class interval

N = Total number of scores
F = frequency
D = x- x

CONCLUSION

This chapter is outlined with the design of the present study and the type and nature of sample. It describes the hypotheses to be tested, the tools employed and the method of administration and scoring. The data collected is analysed and interpreted in the next chapter

❐

19

Analysis and Interpretation of Data

This chapter the classified data are presented in tables and statically analysed. A brief interpretation follows each table. Data was processed in terms of mean and standard deviation.

MEANING OF ANALYSIS

After the data was collected it was classified according to the various categories tabulated and analysed. In short analysis means studying the tabulated material in order to determine facts or meanings. Under ideal conditions of precision and simplicity, analysis present very few problems as the statement of hypotheses and the elaboration of the experimental design will automatically provide for the analysis of the data. The problem raised by the analysis of data is directly related to the complexity of the hypotheses.

TESTING THE HYPOTHESES

Hypothesis: 1

The overall organizational climate of higher secondary school teachers will be Average

TABLE. Showing the Frequency and Percentage of Organizational Climate

Sl.No	Over all Organizational climate	Frequency	Percentage	Cumulative frequency
1.	Low	71	26.01	26.01
2.	Average	129	47.25	73.26
3.	High	73	26.01	100

INTERPRETATION

From the above table it is inferred that the mean of the organizational climate of the scores lying in the average scores. Hence the empirical hypothesis is accepted.

Hypothesis 2.

Over all Job satisfaction of higher secondary school teachers are high

TABLE. Showing the Frequency and Percentage of Job Satisfaction

Sl.No	Job Satisfaction	Frequency	Percentage	Cumulative percentage
1.	Low	73	26.74	26.74
2	Average	129	47.25	73.99
3	High	71	26.74	100
	Total	**273**	**100**	

INTERPRETATION

From the above table it is inferred that the mean score of the job satisfaction is falling in the average category. Hence the empirical hypothesis is rejected.

In order to find out the existence of any significant difference between the number of stay of teachers with regarded to organizational climate the F-ratio was calculated and has been presented in table

Hypothesis: 3

There is no significant difference between the government, aided and private higher secondary schools with regard to their organizational climate.

TABLE: One Way ANOVA showing difference in the mean scores of the Higher Secondary School (Government, Aided and Private) with Respect to the Organizational Climate

Source of variation	D.F	Sum of Square	Mean of Square	F ratio	Level of Significance
Between groups	2	12549.15	6274.57	17.47	0.01
Within groups	270	96963.37	359.12		
Total	**272**	**109512.28**			

Inference

From the above table it is inferred that the calculated F value is greater than the table value and hence there is a significant difference between the Government, aided and private higher secondary schools with regard to their organizational climate at 0.01 level. So further critical ratio will be calculated.

Hypothesis 3a

There will be no significant difference in the organizational climate of Government, Aided and private higher secondary schools

TABLE. Showing the Significance of Difference in the Mean Scores of Government and Aided Higher Secondary Schools with Respect to Organizational Clumate

Type of Management	N	Mean	S.D	SEMD	C.R	L.S
Government	62	166.14	20.06	2.54	0.78	NS
Aided	108	163.68	19.64	1.89		

INTERPRETATION

From above table it is inferred that there is no significant difference in the organizational climate of Government and Aided schools. Hence the null hypothesis is accepted.

TABLE. Showing the Significance of Difference in the Mean Scores of Aided and Private Higher Secondary School with Respect to Organizational Climate

Type of Management	N	Mean	S.D	SEMD	C.R	L.S
Aided	108	163.68	19.64	1.89	5.05	0.01
Private	103	150.72	17.46	1.72		

INTERPRETATION

From above table it is inferred that there is a significant difference in the organizational climate of Aided and private schools. Hence the empirical hypothesis is accepted.

TABLE. Showing the Significance of Difference in the Mean Scores of Government and Private Higher Secondary Schools with Respect to Organizational Climate

Type of Management	N	Mean	S.D	SEMD	C.R	L.S
Government	62	166.14	20.06	2.548	5.19	0.01
Private	103	150.72	17.46	1.72		

INTERPRETATION

From above table it is inferred that there is a significant difference in the organizational climate of Government and private schools. Hence the empirical hypothesis is accepted.

In order to find out the existence of any significant difference between the number of stay of teachers with regarded to organizational climate the F-ratio was calculated and has been presented in table

Hypothesis: 4

There is no significant difference between the government, aided and private higher secondary school teachers with regard to the job satisfaction

TABLE: One Way ANOVA Showing Sifference in the Mean Scores of the Higher Secondary School Teachers (Government, Aided and Private) with Respect to their job Satisfaction.

Source of variation	D.F	Sum of Square	Mean of Square	F ratio	Level of Significance
Between groups	2	5190.28	2595.14	3.54	0.01
Within groups	270	197746.99	732.39		
Total	**272**	**202937.28**			

Inference

From the above table it is inferred that the calculated F value is greater than the table value and hence there is a significant difference between the Government, aided and private higher secondary school teachers with respect to their job satisfaction at 0.01 level. So further critical ratio will be calculated.

Hypothesis 4a

There will be no significant difference in the job satisfaction of Government and Aided higher secondary schools

TABLE: Showing the Significance of Difference in the Mean Scores of Higher Secondary School Teachers of Government and Aided schools with Respect to the Job Satisfaction

Type of Management	N	Mean	S.D	SEMD	C.R	L.S
Government	62	256.06	26.04	3.30	2.67	0.05
Aided	108	244.68	27.17	2.61		

INTERPRETATION

From above table it is inferred that there is a significant difference in the job satisfaction of Government and Aided schools. Hence the null hypothesis is rejected.

TABLE. Showing the Significance of Difference in the Mean Scores of Higher Secondary School Teachers of Aided and Private Schools with Respect to the Job Satisfaction

Type of Management	N	Mean	S.D	SEMD	C.R	L.S
Aided	108	244.68	27.17	2.61	1.42	NS
Private	103	250.01	27.54	2.71		

INTERPRETATION

From above table it is inferred that there is no significant difference in the job satisfaction of Aided and private schools. Hence the null hypothesis is accepted.

TABLE: Showing the significance of difference in the mean scores of higher secondary school teachers of government and private schools with respect to job satisfaction

Type of Management	N	Mean	S.D	SEMD	C.R	L.S
Government	62	256.06	26.04	3.30	1.39	NS
Private	103	250.01	27.54	2.71		

INTERPRETATION

From the above table it is inferred that there is no significant difference in the organizational climate of Government and private schools. Hence the null hypothesis is accepted.

Hypothesis 5

There will be no significant difference in the organizational climate of higher secondary school teachers with respect to the gender

TABLE: Showing the Significance of Difference in the Mean of Organizational Climate Test Scores of Male and Female Higher Secondary School Teachers

Gender	N	Mean	S.D	SEMD	C.R	L.S
Male	118	156.71	17.94	1.65	1.91	NS
Female	155	161.36	21.38	1.71		

INTERPRETATION

From above table it is found that there is no significant difference in the organizational climate of higher secondary school teachers with respect to their gender. Hence the null hypothesis is accepted.

Hypothesis 6

There will be no significant difference in the Job satisfaction of higher secondary school teachers with respect to the gender

TABLE: Showing the Significance of Difference in the Mean of Job Satisfaction Test Scores of Male and Female Higher Secondary School Teachers.

Gender	N	Mean	S.D	SEMD	C.R	L.S
Male	118	243.38	27.47	2.52	3.17	0.01
Female	155	253.77	26.40	2.12		

INTERPRETATION

From above table it is found that there is a significant difference in the organizational climate of higher secondary school teachers with respect to their gender. Hence the null hypothesis is rejected.

The findings are graphically represented in figure

Hypothesis 7

There will be no significant difference in the organizational climate of higher secondary school teachers with respect to the locale

TABLE: Showing the significance of difference in the mean of organizational climate test scores of higher secondary school teachers with respect to the locale

Locale	N	Mean	S.D	SEMD	C.R	L.S
Urban	167	157.0.9	20.67	1.60	2.35	0.05
Rural	106	162.91	18.60	1.80		

INTERPRETATION

From above table it is inferred that there is a significant difference in the organizational climate of higher secondary school teachers with respect to the locale. Hence the null hypothesis is rejected.

Hypothesis 8

There will be no significant difference in the Job satisfaction of higher secondary school teachers with respect to the locale.

TABLE: Showing the Significance of Difference in the Mean of Job Satisfaction Test Scores of Higher Secondary School Teachers with Respect to the Locale

Locale	N	Mean	S.D	SEMD	C.R	L.S
Urban	167	249.08	26.35	2.04	0.15	NS
Rural	106	249.59	28.88	2.80		

INTERPRETATION

From above table it is inferred that there is no significant difference in the job satisfaction of higher secondary school teachers with respect to the locale. Hence the null hypothesis is accepted.

In order to find out the existence of any significant difference between the number of stay of teachers with regarded to organizational climate the F-ratio was calculated and has been presented in table

Hypothesis

There is no significant difference between the organizational climate of higher secondary school teachers with regard to their age.

TABLE: One Way ANOVA Showing Difference in the Mean Scores of Organizational Climate of the Higher Secondary School Teachers with Respect to their Age.

Source of variation	D.F	Sum of Square	Mean of Square	F ratio	Level of Significance
Between groups	2	392.98	196.49	0.48	NS
Within groups	270	109119.54	404.14		
Total	**272**	**109512.53**			

Inference

From the above table it is inferred that the calculated F value is not greater than the table value and hence there is no significant difference between the organizational climate of higher secondary school teachers with regard to their age. Hence the null hypothesis is accepted and further analysis has been undertaken to see group difference in the following table.

In order to find out the existence of any significant difference between the number of stay of teachers with regarded to job satisfaction the F-ratio was calculated and has been presented in table.

Hypothesis

There is no significant difference between the job satisfaction of higher secondary school teachers with regard to their age.

TABLE: One Way ANOVA Showing Difference in the Mean Scores of Job Satisfaction of the Higher Secondary School Teachers with Respect to their Age.

Source of variation	D.F	Sum of Square	Mean of Square	F ratio	Level of Significance
Between groups	2	392.98	196.49	0.48	NS
Within groups	270	109119.54	404.14		
Total	272	109512.53			

Inference

From the above table it is inferred that the calculated F value is not greater than the table value and hence there is no significant difference between the job satisfaction of higher secondary school teachers with regard to their age. Hence the null hypothesis is accepted.

In order to find out the existence of any significant difference between the number of stay of teachers with regarded to organizational climate the F-ratio was calculated and has been presented in table

Hypothesis

There is no significant difference between the organizational climate of higher secondary school teachers with regard to the no of years of stay in the present school.

TABLE: One Way ANOVA Showing Difference in the Mean Scores of Organizational Climate of the Higher Secondary School Teachers with Respect to the no of Years Stay in the Present School.

Source of variation	D.F	Sum of Square	Mean of Square	F ratio	Level of Significance
Between groups	2	211.68	105.84	.26	NS
Within groups	270	109300.84	404.81		
Total	**272**	**109512.53**			

Inference

From the above table it is inferred that the calculated F value is not greater than the table value and hence there is no significant difference between the organizational climate of higher secondary school teachers with regard to the no of years of stay in the present school. Hence the null hypothesis is accepted.

In order to find out the existence of any significant difference between the number of stay of teachers with regarded to organizational climate the F-ratio was calculated and has been presented in table

Hypothesis

There is no significant difference between the job satisfactions of higher secondary school teachers with regard to the no of years of stay in the present school.

TABLE: One Way ANOVA Showing Difference in the Mean Scores of Job Satisfaction of the Higher Secondary School Teachers with Respect to the no of Years Stay in the Present School

Source of variation	D.F	Sum of Square	Mean of Square	F ratio	Level of Significance
Between groups	2	5413.19	2706.59	3.6	0.01
Within groups	270	197524.08	731.57		
Total	**272**	**202937.28**			

Inference

From the above table it is inferred that the calculated F value is greater than the table value and hence there is a significant difference between the job satisfaction of higher secondary school teachers with regard to the number of years stay in the present school at 0.01 level. Hence the null hypothesis is rejected.

Hypothesis

There will be no significant difference in the Job satisfaction of higher secondary school teachers with related to the number of years of stay in the present school

TABLE: Showing the Significance of Difference in the Mean of Job Satisfaction test Scores of Higher Secondary School Teachers Stayed in the Present School up to 5 and 5 – 10 years

Locale	N	Mean	S.D	SEMD	C.R	L.S
Less than 5 years	72	255.51	26.93	3.17	1.51	NS
5 to 10 years	114	249.52	25.94	2.43		

INTERPRETATION

From above table it is inferred that there is no significant difference in the Job satisfaction of higher secondary school teachers stayed in the present school up to 5 and 5 to 10 years. Hence the null hypothesis is accepted.

TABLE: Showing the Significance of Difference in the Mean job Satisfaction test Scores of Higher Secondary School Teachers Stayed in the Present School of Less than 5 years and above 10 years

Locale	N	Mean	S.D	SEMD	C.R	L.S
Less than 5 years	72	255.51	26.93	3.17	2.64	0.01
Above 10 years	87	243.80	28.52	3.05		

INTERPRETATION

From above table it is inferred that there is a significant difference in the job satisfaction of higher secondary school teachers stayed in the present school up to 5 and above 10 years. Hence the null hypothesis is rejected

TABLE: Showing the Significance of Difference in the Mean of Job Satisfaction Test Scores of Higher Secondary School Teachers Stayed in the Present School up to 5-10 years and above 10years

Locale	N	Mean	S.D	SEMD	C.R	L.S
5 to 10 years	114	249.52	25.94	2.43	1.48	NS
Above 10 years	87	243.80	28.52	3.05		

INTERPRETATION

From above table it is inferred that there is no significant difference in the job satisfaction of higher secondary school teachers stayed in the present school up to having 5 to 10 years and above 10. Hence the null hypothesis is accepted.

ANOVA org climate vs. monthly salary

In order to find out the existence of any significant difference between Salary of the month of higher secondary school teachers with regarded to organizational climate, the F-ratio was calculated and it has been presented in table

Results of ANOVA for organizational climate with respect to the monthly salary of higher secondary school teachers.

Hypothesis

There is no significant difference between the salary of the month of higher secondary school teachers with regard to the organizational climate.

TABLE: One Way ANOVA Showing Difference in the Mean Scores of the Salary of the Month of Higher Secondary School Teachers with Regard to the Organizational Climate

Source of variation	D.F	Sum of Square	Mean of Square	F ratio	Level of Significance
Between groups	2	12030.45	6015.22	16.66	0.01
Within groups	270	97482.07	361.04		
Total	**272**	**109512.53**			

Inference

From the above table it is inferred that the calculated F value is greater than the table value and hence there is a significant difference between the salary of the month of higher secondary school teachers with regard to the organizational climate at 0.01 level. Hence the null hypothesis is rejected.

Hypothesis

There will be no significant difference in the organizational climate of higher secondary school teachers with related to their monthly salary

TABLE: Showing the Significance of Difference in the Mean of Organizational Climate test Scores of Higher Secondary School Teachers Having the Salary Range of up to 7,500 and 7,500 to 15,000 per month

Locale	N	Mean	S.D	SEMD	C.R	L.S
Up to 7,500	81	149.14	17.87	1.98	5.36	0.01
7,500 to 15,000	131	163.60	19.78	1.72		

INTERPRETATION

From above table it is inferred that there is a significant difference in the organizational climate of higher secondary school teachers having the salary range of up to 7,500 and 7,500 to 15,000 per month. Hence the null hypothesis is rejected.

TABLE: Showing the significance of difference in the mean of organizational climate test scores of higher secondary school teachers having the salary range of 7,500 to 15,000 and above 15,000 per month

Locale	N	Mean	S.D	SEMD	C.R	L.S
7,500 to 15,000	131	163.60	19.78	2.09	2.04	0.05
Above 15,000	61	163.82	18.74	1.95		

INTERPRETATION

From above table it is inferred that there is a significant difference in the organizational climate of higher secondary school teachers having the salary range of 7,500 to 15,000 and above 15,000 per month. Hence the null hypothesis is rejected.

TABLE: Showing the significance of difference in the mean of organizational climate test scores of higher secondary school teachers having the salary range of up to 7,500 and above 15,000 per month

Locale	N	Mean	S.D	SEMD	C.R	L.S
Up to 7,500	81	149.14	17.87	1.98	4.75	0.01
Above 15,000	61	163.82	18.74	2.39		

INTERPRETATION

From above table it is inferred that there is a significant difference in the organizational climate of higher secondary school teachers having the salary range of up to 7,500 and above 15,000 per month. Hence the null hypothesis is rejected.

ANOVA job satisfaction vs. monthly salary

In order to find out the existence of any significant difference between Salary of the month of higher secondary school teachers with regarded to their job satisfaction the F-ratio was calculated and it has been presented in table

Results of ANOVA for monthly salary of higher secondary school teachers with respect to their job satisfaction.

Hypothesis

There is no significant difference between the salary of the month of higher secondary school teachers with regard to their job satisfaction.

TABLE: One Way ANOVA Showing Difference in the Mean Scores of the Salary of the Month of Higher Secondary School Teachers with Regard to the Job Satisfaction

Source of variation	D.F	Sum of Square	Mean of Square	F ratio	Level of Significance
Between groups	2	60.68	30.34	0.04	NS
Within groups	270	202876.59	751.39		
Total	**272**	**202937.28**			

Inference

From the above table it is inferred that the calculated F value is greater than the table value and hence there is a significant difference between the salary of the month of higher secondary school teachers with regard to the job satisfaction. Hence the null hypothesis is rejected.

ANOVA organizational climate vs. Length of total experience

In order to find out the existence of any significant difference between the length of total experience with regarded to the organizational climate of higher secondary school teachers, the F-ratio was calculated and it has been presented in table

Hypothesis

There is no significant difference between the organizational climate with respect to the length of experience of higher secondary school teachers

TABLE: One Way ANOVA Showing Difference in the Mean Scores of the Salary of the Month of Higher Secondary School Teachers with Regard to the Organizational Climate

Source of variation	D.F	Sum of Square	Mean of Square	F ratio	Level of Significance
Between groups	2	3601.70	1800.85	4.59	0.01
Within groups	270	105910.83	392.26		
Total	**272**	**109512.53**			

Inference

From the above table it is inferred that the calculated F value is greater than the table value and hence there is a significant difference between the salary of the month of higher secondary school teachers with regard to their organizational climate. Hence the null hypothesis is rejected.

Hypothesis

There will be no significant difference in the organizational climate of higher secondary school teachers with respect to their length of experience

TABLE: Showing the Significance of Difference in the Mean of Organizational Climate Test Scores of Higher Secondary School Teachers with Respect to their Length of Experience of less than 5 and 6 – 15 years

Locale	N	Mean	S.D	SEMD	C.R	L.S
Less than 5 years	72	159.40	18.72	2.20	1.01	NS
6 to 15 years	138	156.47	20.63	1.75		

INTERPRETATION

From above table it is inferred that there is no significant difference in the organizational climate of higher secondary school teachers with respect to their length of experience of less than 5 and 6 – 15 years. Hence the null hypothesis is accepted.

TABLE: Showing the Significance of Difference in the Mean of Organizational Climate test Scores of Higher Secondary School Teachers with Respect to their Length of Experience of Less than 5 and above 15 years

Locale	N	Mean	S.D	SEMD	C.R	L.S
Less than 5 years	72	159.40	18.72	2.20	1.90	NS
Above 15 years	63	165.60	19.11	2.40		

INTERPRETATION

From above table it is inferred that there is no significant difference in the organizational climate of higher secondary school teachers with respect to their length of experience of less than 5 and above 15 years. Hence the null hypothesis is accepted.

TABLE: Showing the Significance of Difference in the Mean of Organizational Climate test Scores of Higher Secondary School Teachers with Respect to their Length of Experience Between 6 to 15 years and above 15 years

Locale	N	Mean	S.D	SEMD	C.R	L.S
6-15 years	138	156.47	20.63	1.75	2.97	0.01
Above 15 years	63	165.60	19.11	2.40		

INTERPRETATION

From above table it is inferred that there is a significant difference in the organizational climate of higher secondary school teachers with respect to their length of experience between 6 to 15 years and above 15 years at 0.01 level. Hence the null hypothesis is rejected.

ANOVA organizational climate vs. Length of total experience

In order to find out the existence of any significant difference between the length of total experience with regarded to the job satisfaction of higher secondary school teachers, the F-ratio was calculated and it has been presented in table

Hypothesis

There is no significant difference between the job satisfaction with respect to the length of experience of higher secondary school teachers

TABLE: One Way ANOVA Showing Difference in the Mean Scores of the Salary of the Month of Higher Secondary School Teachers with Regard to the Job Satisfaction

Source of variation	D.F	Sum of Square	Mean of Square	F ratio	Level of Significance
Between groups	2	6778.73	3389.36	4.66	0.01
Within groups	270	196158.55	726.51		
Total	**272**	**202937.28**			

Inference

From the above table it is inferred that the calculated F value is greater than the table value and hence there is a significant difference between the salary of the month of higher secondary school teachers with regard to their job satisfaction. Hence the null hypothesis is rejected.

Hypothesis

There will be no significant difference in the job satisfaction of higher secondary school teachers with respect to their length of experience

TABLE: Showing the Significance of Difference in the Mean of Job Satisfaction test Scores of Higher Secondary School Teachers with Respect to their Length of Experience of less than 5 and 6 – 15 years.

Locale	N	Mean	S.D	SEMD	C.R	L.S
Less than 5 years	72	255.63	28.67	3.37	2.83	0.01
6 to 15 years	138	244.47	26.34	2.24		

INTERPRETATION

From above table it is inferred that there is a significant difference in the job satisfaction of higher secondary school teachers with respect to their length of experience of less than 5 and 6 – 15 years. Hence the null hypothesis is rejected.

TABLE: Showing the significance of difference in the mean of job satisfaction test scores of higher secondary school teachers with respect to their length of experience of less than 5 and above 15 years

Locale	N	Mean	S.D	SEMD	C.R	L.S
Less than 5 years	72	255.63	28.67	3.37	0.65	NS
Above 15 years	63	252.55	26.24	3.30		

INTERPRETATION

From above table it is inferred that there is no significant difference in the job satisfaction of higher secondary school teachers with respect to their length of experience of less than 5 and above 15 years. Hence the null hypothesis is accepted.

TABLE: Showing the Significance of Difference in the Mean of job Satisfaction Test Scores of Higher Secondary School Teachers with Respect to their length of Experience Between 6 to 15 years and above 15 years

Locale	N	Mean	S.D	SEMD	C.R	L.S
6-15 years	138	244.47	26.34	2.24	2.02	0.05
Above 15 years	63	252.55	26.24	3.30		

INTERPRETATION

From above table it is inferred that there is a significant difference in the job satisfaction of higher secondary school teachers with respect to their length of experience between 6 to 15 years and above 15 years at 0.01 level. Hence the null hypothesis is rejected.

Chi-square test

Hypothesis

There is a significant relationship between the overall organizational climates with respect to the different type of schools

TABLE: Showing Chi Square test Between the Overall Organizational Climate with Respect to the Type of School Chi Square Test

Variable		Organizational climate				Chi square	L.S
		Low	Average	High	Total		
Type of School	Government	10	31	21	62	24.26	0.01
	Aided	22	46	40	108		
	Private	39	52	12	103		

Interpretation

From the above table it is clearly understood that the calculated chi-square value is more than table value and therefore there is a positive relationship between the organizational climate and the different type of schools. Hence the empirical hypothesis is accepted.

Hypothesis

There is a significant relationship between the overall organizational climates with respect to the locality of schools.

TABLE: Showing chi square test between the overall organizational climate with respect to the locality of school Chi square test.

Variable		Organizational climate				Chi square	L.S
		Low	Average	High	Total		
Locality of Schools	Rural	52	79	36	167	8.67	0.01
	Urban	19	50	37	106		

Interpretation

From the above table it is clearly understood that the calculated chi-square value is more than table value and therefore there is a positive relationship between the organizational climate and the locality of schools. Hence the empirical hypothesis is accepted.

Hypothesis

There is a significant relationship between the overall organizational climates with respect to the gender of higher secondary school teachers

TABLE: Showing chi square test between the overall organizational climate with respect to the gender of higher secondary school teachers Chi square test

Variable		Organizational climate				Chi square	L.S
		Low	Average	High	Total		
Gender	Male	36	57	25	118	4.06	NS
	Female	35	72	48	155		

Interpretation

From the above table it is clearly understood that the calculated chi-square value is less than table value and therefore there is no relationship between the organizational climate and the gender of the higher secondary school teachers. Hence the empirical hypothesis is rejected.

Hypothesis

There is a significant relationship between the overall organizational climates with respect to the age group of higher secondary school teachers

TABLE: Showing Chi Square test Between the Overall Organizational Climate with Respect to the Age Group of Higher Secondary School Teachers Chi Square test

Variable		Organizational climate				Chi square	L.S
		Low	Average	High	Total		
Age (in Years)	Below 35	21	43	17	81	2.74	NS
	35-45	29	51	30	110		
	45 and above	21	35	26	82		

Interpretation

From the above table it is clearly understood that the calculated chi-square value is less than table value and therefore there is no relationship between the organizational climate and the age group of the higher secondary school teachers. Hence the empirical hypothesis is rejected.

Hypothesis

There is a significant relationship between the overall organizational climates with respect to the Number of years stay in the present school of the higher secondary school teachers

TABLE: Showing chi square test between the overall organizational climate with respect to Number of years stay in the present school of the higher secondary school teachers Chi square test

Variable		Organizational climate				Chi square	L.S
		Low	Average	High	Total		
No of Years stay in the present school	Up to 5	17	40	15	72	4.32	NS
	5 to 10	34	47	33	114		
	10 and above	20	42	25	87		

Interpretation

From the above table it is clearly understood that the calculated chi-square value is less than table value and therefore there is no relationship between the organizational climate and Number of years stay in the present school of the higher secondary school teachers. Hence the empirical hypothesis is rejected.

Hypothesis

There is a significant relationship between the overall organizational climate with respect to the Salary of the month of the higher secondary school teachers.

TABLE: Showing chi square test between the overall organizational climate with respect to the salary of the month of the higher secondary school teachers Chi square test

Variable		Organizational climate				Chi square	L.S
		Low	Average	High	Total		
Salary of the month (In Rs)	Up to 7,500	34	39	8	81	25.78	0.01
	7500-15,000	24	66	41	131		
	15,000 & above	13	24	24	61		

Interpretation

From the above table it is clearly understood that the calculated chi-square value is more than table value and therefore there is a positive relationship between the organizational climate and salary of the month of the higher secondary school teachers. Hence the empirical hypothesis is accepted.

Hypothesis

There is a significant relationship between the overall organizational climate with respect to the total years of experience of the higher secondary school teachers

TABLE: Showing chi square test between the overall organizational climate with respect to the total years of experience of the higher secondary school teachers Chi square test

Variable		Organizational climate				Chi square	L.S
		Low	Average	High	Total		
Total Years of experience	Up to 5	17	39	16	72	9.49	0.05
	6 to 15	44	61	33	138		
	15 and above	10	29	24	63		

Interpretation

From the above table it is clearly understood that the calculated chi-square value is more than table value and therefore there is a positive relationship between the organizational climate and the total years of experience of the higher secondary school teachers. Hence the empirical hypothesis is accepted.

Hypothesis

There is a significant relationship between the job satisfactions of higher secondary school teachers with respect to the type of schools

TABLE: Showing Chi Square test Between the Job Satisfactions of Higher Secondary School Teachers with Respect to the Type of Schools Chi Square Test

Variable		Job Satisfaction				Chi square	L.S
		Low	**Average**	**High**	**Total**		
Type of school	Government	13	29	20	62	4.04	NS
	Aided	30	56	44	108		
	Matriculation	30	44	29	103		

Interpretation

From the above table it is clearly understood that the calculated chi-square value is less than table value and therefore there is a no relationship between the job satisfaction of higher secondary school teachers with respect to the type of schools. Hence the empirical hypothesis is rejected.

Hypothesis

There is a significant relationship between the job satisfactions of higher secondary school teachers with respect to the locality of schools

TABLE: Showing Chi Square test Between the l Job Satisfaction of Higher Secondary School Teachers with Respect to the locality of School Chi Square Test

Variable		Organizational climate				Chi square	L.S
		Low	**Average**	**High**	**Total**		
Locality of Schools	Rural	45	80	42	167	9.43	0.01
	Urban	28	49	29	106		

Interpretation

From the above table it is clearly understood that the calculated chi-square value is more than the table value and therefore there is a positive relationship between the job satisfaction of higher secondary school teachers with respect to the locality of schools.Hence the empirical hypothesis is accepted.

Hypothesis

There is a significant relationship between the job satisfaction of higher secondary school teachers with respect to the gender

TABLE: Showing Chi Square Test Between the Job Satisfaction of the Higher Secondary School Teachers with Respect to the Gender of Higher Secondary School Teachers Chi square Test

Variable		Organizational climate				Chi square	L.S
		Low	Average	High	Total		
Gender	Male	44	52	22	118	13.42	0.05
	Female	29	77	49	155		

Interpretation

From the above table it is clearly understood that the calculated chi-square value is more than table value and therefore there is a positive relationship between the job satisfaction and the gender of the higher secondary school teachers. Hence the empirical hypothesis is accepted.

Hypothesis

There is a significant relationship between the job satisfactions with respect to the age group of higher secondary school teachers

TABLE: Showing chi square test between the job satisfaction with respect to the age group of higher secondary school teachers Chi square test

Variable		Organizational climate				Chi square	L.S
		Low	Average	High	Total		
Age (in Years)	Below 35	26	28	27	81	9.74	NS
	35-45	30	59	21	110		
	45 and above	17	42	23	82		

Interpretation

From the above table it is clearly understood that the calculated chi-square value is less than table value and therefore there is no relationship between the job satisfaction and the age group of the higher secondary school teachers. Hence the empirical hypothesis is rejected.

Hypothesis

There is a significant relationship between the Jobs satisfactions with respect to the Number of years stay in the present school of the higher secondary school teachers

TABLE: Showing Chi Square Test Between the l Job Satisfaction with Respect to Number of Years Stay in the Present School of the Higher Secondary School Teachers Chi Square Test

Variable		Organizational climate				Chi square	L.S
		Low	Average	High	Total		
No of Years stay in the present school	Up to 5	18	28	26	72	6.09	0.01
	5 to 10	29	60	25	114		
	10 and above	26	41	20	87		

Interpretation

From the above table it is clearly understood that the calculated chi-square value is more than the table value and therefore there is a positive relationship between the job satisfaction and Number of years stay in the present school of higher secondary school teachers. Hence the empirical hypothesis is accepted.

Hypothesis

There is a significant relationship between the job satisfactions with respect to the Salary of the month of the higher secondary school teachers

TABLE: Showing Chi Square Test Between the Job Satisfaction with Respect to the Salary of the Month of the Higher Secondary School Teachers Chi Square Test

Variable		Organizational climate				Chi square	L.S
		Low	Average	High	Total		
Salary of the month (In Rs)	Up to 7,500	26	32	23	81	5.55	NS
	7500-15,000	35	61	35	131		
	15,000 & above	12	36	13	61		

Interpretation

From the above table it is clearly understood that the calculated chi-square value is less than table value and therefore there is no relationship between the job satisfaction and salary of the month of higher secondary school teachers. Hence the empirical hypothesis is rejected.

Hypothesis

There is a significant relationship between the job satisfactions with respect to the total years of experience of higher secondary school teachers

TABLE: Showing chi square test between the job satisfaction with respect to the total years of experience of the higher secondary school teachers Chi square test

Variable		Organizational climate				Chi square	L.S
		Low	Average	High	Total		
Total Years of experience	Up to 5	18	27	27	72	15.77	0.01
	6 to 15	46	67	25	138		
	15 and above	9	35	19	63		

Interpretation

From the above table it is clearly understood that the calculated chi-square value is more than table value and therefore there is a positive relationship between the job satisfaction and the total years of experience of higher secondary school teachers. Hence the empirical hypothesis is accepted.

Hypothesis

There is a significant relationship between the overall organizational climates with respect to the job satisfaction of the higher secondary school teachers.

TABLE: Showing Chi Square Test Between the Overall Organizational Climate with Respect to the Job Satisfaction of the Higher Secondary School Teachers Chi Square Test

Variable		Organizational climate				Chi square	L.S
		Low	Average	High	Total		
Job satisfaction	Low	32	28	11	71	24.01	0.01
	Average	34	60	35	129		
	High	7	41	25	73		

Interpretation

From the above table it is clearly understood that the calculated chi-square value is more than table value and therefore there is a positive relationship between the organizational climate and the job satisfaction of the higher secondary school teachers. Hence the empirical hypothesis is accepted. Correlation coefficient

❐

20

Summary, Findings and Conclusion

Research is not only compiling counting and tabulating the consequences of hypothesis rather it is the careful observation, enquiry and application of rigorous logic. Research is a process of testing rather than providing, hence the investigator listed this finding in this chapter.

OBJECTIVES

1. To study the organizational climate of schools under different types of school management
2. To study the significant difference between the organizational climate with regard to the Gender
3. To study the significant difference between the organizational climate with regard to the Locale of the School
4. To study the significant difference between the organizational climate with regard to the Age of the higher secondary school teachers
5. To study the significant difference between the organizational climate with respect to the Number of years stay in the present school
6. To study the significant difference between the organizational climate with respect to the monthly salary
7. To study the significant difference between the organizational climate with respect to the total experience

8. To study the level of job satisfaction of higher secondary school teachers
9. To study the level of job satisfaction of higher secondary school teacher with regard to the gender
10. To study the level of job satisfaction of higher secondary school teacher with regard to the Locale of the school
11. To study the level of job satisfaction of higher secondary school teacher with regard to the Age
12. To study the level of job satisfaction of higher secondary school teacher with regard to the Number of years stay in the present school
13. To study the level of job satisfaction of higher secondary school teacher with regard to the monthly salary
14. To study the level of job satisfaction of higher secondary school teacher with respect to their total experience
15. To study the relationship between organizational climate and job satisfaction of higher secondary school teachers

SAMPLE

The study consists of 275 higher secondary school teachers spread over fifteen schools in Madurai. The sample represents Higher Secondary teachers belonging to different types of schools like government, private and aided. Hence the sample is a stratified random sample.

TOOLS AND MATERIALS USED

To verify the different types of hypothesis framed, the following tools were used.

Organizational climate

Job satisfaction

MAJOR FINDINGS OF THE STUDY

The overall organizational climate of higher secondary school teachers is moderate

There is a significant difference in the organizational climate of schools under different types of management.

There is a significant difference in the organizational climate of aided and government higher secondary schools

There is a significant difference in the Organizational Climate of aided and private higher secondary schools.

There is a significant difference in the organizational climate of Government and private higher secondary schools

Gender has no bearing on the level of organizational climate of higher secondary school teachers.

There is a significant difference in the organizational climate of schools with respect to the locale

Age has no bearing on the level of organizational climate of higher secondary school teachers

There is no significant difference in the organizational climate of schools with respect to the no of years stay of teachers in the present schools

There is a significant difference in the organizational climate of schools with respect to the salary of teachers

There is a significant difference in the level of organizational climate of higher secondary school teachers with respect to their length of experience

There is a significant difference in the level of job satisfaction of higher secondary school teachers under different types of management

There is a significant difference in the level of job satisfaction of aided and government higher secondary schools

There is a significant difference in the level of job satisfaction of aided and private higher secondary schools.

There is a significant difference in the level of job satisfaction of Government and private higher secondary schools

Gender has a bearing on the level of job satisfaction of higher secondary school teachers.

There is no significant difference in the job satisfaction of schools with respect to the locale

Age has no bearing on the level of job satisfaction of higher secondary school teachers

There is a significant difference in the level of job satisfaction of higher secondary school teachers with respect to the no of years stay in the present schools

There is no significant difference in the job satisfaction higher secondary school teachers with respect to the salary

There is a significant difference in the level of job satisfaction of higher secondary school teachers with respect to their length of experience

There is a significant positive correlation between organizational climate and job satisfaction of higher Secondary school teachers.

❒

Bibliography

1. Adinarayan, S.P. and Rajamanickam M. "*A Study of Student Attitude towards Religion, the Spiritual and the Supernatural*". Journal of Social Psychology, 1962, Vol.57 (1), pp.105-111.
2. Boerce, C.G. (2001) Anxiety Hall C.S. (1954) "*A Primer of Freudian Psychology*", Cleveland: World.
3. Boisvert, Donad Luc (1990), "*Religion and Nationalism in Qubec the saint – Jean – Baptiste celebrations in socioligical perspective*", Dissertation Abstract Internationalm, Vol-52 (11), May 1992, P.3964.
4. Deonandam, Kalowatie (1990), *"Religion and the struggle for hegemony in Nicaragua",* Dissertation Abstract International, Vol.52 (11) May 1992, p.4070A.
5. Deonandem, Kalowetie (1990), *"Religion and the struggle for hegemony in Nicaragua",* Dissertation Abstract International, Vol. 52(11) May 1992, PP 4070 A.
6. Dutt N.K (1965), *"Attitude of the University students towards religion",* Journal of Psychological Research. 1965, Vol.9(3), pp.127-130.
7. Francis, Leslie J(1993), *"Personality and Religion among college students in the U.K. Personality and Individual differences,"* April 1993 Vol.14 (4), pp.619-622.
8. Freud (1955), Analysis of phobia in a five year – old Boy. London: Hogarth Press, Vol.10.
9. Gaston, J.E. and Broun, L.B. Religion and Gender Proto type. Psychological abstracts 1993, Vol. 80, 9382.
10. Green Celia (2004) betters from Exile: Observations on a culture in decline, Oxford Forum, Chapter –I, xx.

11. Greer J.E. "*Attitude to religion reconsidered*", British Journal of Educational Students, Vol.31, No. 1, pp. 18-28.
12. Gupta A. (1980), "*Personality and Mental consistent of Religiousness in the Tibetan Students in the Adolescent Age Group*", Buch M.B., third survey of research in education.
13. Hassan M.K. and Khalique (1981), "*Religiosity and its correlates in college students*", Journal of Psychological Research, Vol.25 (3), pp.129-136.
14. Helpburm, Lawrence R. Religion in the social studies. The question of religious attitudes, Religious education, 1971, (May) Vol. 66 (3),172 – 179.
15. Horne, E.P. & Stender, W.H. Students Attitude to Religious practicies Journal of Social Psychology (21) 1945, p. 215.
16. John Kottman E. A semantic study of some selected demensions of religous attitude, sociology and social research, 1968, 52(4), 430-437.
17. Kapil, H.K. and Agarwal, Susham, changing patterns of volves amongst women in modern Hindu Society. Psychological Research, 1967, 2(1-2), 29-32.
18. Krause, Neal (1993), "*Measuring Religiosity in their life*", Vol.15 (2), pp.170-197.
19. Lester. D.Crow & Alice Crow, "*Educational Psychology*", New Delhi: Publishers: Eurassa Publishing House Pvt. Ltd., Ramnagar, pp.241-242.
20. Lewis, Robert E, Eraser Make W and Pecora, Peter J. "*religiosity among Indochinese Students in Utah*", Journal for scientific study of religion, June, 1988, Vol. 27(2), pp. 272-283.
21. Loewerthal, Kate M and Goldblatt, Vivienne, "*Family size and depressive symptoms in orthodox Jewish Women*" Journal of Psychiatric research 1993 (Jan – Mar) Vol. 27(1), pp. 3-10.
22. Maranell, Cary M. Factor analytic study of some selected dimensions of relilgous attitude sociology and social research, 1968, 52(4) 430-437.
23. Mary, R. (1950), "*The meaning of Anxiety*", New York: Ronald.
24. Medoof, M.H. & Skow, L. Lee, Religion and behaviour, An emperical analysis Psychological Abstracts, 1993, Vol. 80, 13254.
25. Misra S.L (1970), "*A Comparative study of religion – caste difference in concept formation ability of young adult*", Psychological annual Vol.4, pp.10-12.

26. Nagarajan K. (1994), "*Research methodology in Education* Chennai: Sterling Publishers Pvt.Ltd., pp.354-355.
27. Pang, Henry, Religious attitude of students, Psychological reports, 1968, 22(2), 344.
28. Ponton, Marcel.O, and Gorsuch, Richer.L (1995), "*Prejudice and religion revisited; A cross-cultural investigation with a venezuelan sample*", Journal for the scientific study of religion Vol.27 92), pp.260-271.
29. Prizyna, Wlady Slaw. Religious attitude and personality traits analysed on the basis of dera supplied by RB cattel's 16 factor questionnaire. Rocniki Filozoficzne: Anaales de philosophie, 1969, Vol. 17(4), 99-124.
30. Rajamanickam (1966), "*A psychological study of religious and related attitudes of the students and professional groups in South India*", Annamalai: Annamalai University.
31. Rizvi S.A.H. (1986), "*A study of attitude towards religion education in relation to certain valve orientations Buch.* M.B. Forth Survey of research in education, 1991, pp. 190.
32. Roquiya Zainuddin (1994), "*Religiosity and Spirituality as related to some personality needs*", Journal of community and research, Vol.2(2), pp.105-114.
33. Sayed Firoj and Karananidhi S., "*A study of religiosity and valves, Journal of Psychological research",* 1995, Vol. 39 (3), pp. 30-34.
34. Seetharam G.K.N., *"It is time to act to the values,"* Yojana 30(1-2) 1986 pp.73-76.
35. Seligman, M.E.P., Walker, E.F. & Rosenhan, D.L. (2001) Abnormal Psychology, (4th end) New York, W.W. Norton & Company, Inc.
36. Spielberger, C.D. (1966), The effects of Anxiety on complex learning is academic achievement", New York: Academic Press.
37. Swami Nikhilanda "Inter – religious attitude; Rama Krishna Vivekandnada Centre, New York.
38. Tandom B.K (1967) "*A study of attitude towards religion of Higher Secondary School students in Utterpradesh towns",* Buch M.B. A survey of research in education, pp. 132.
39. Telford, C.W. A study of religious attitude: Journal of social Psychology 31, 1950, p. 217-230.
40. Thomas Thai. V. An investigation of religious attitudes, ideals, and personality trafts of the four groups of Catholic College Student Dissertational Abstract International, 1969, 30 (4-4), 1441.

41. Tritter, - Jonathan (1992), "*An Educated change in; Moral Values some Effects of Religious and State Schools on their Students,*" Oxford – Review-of-Education; Vol.18, No.1, pp.29-43.
42. Wiema, J. Authoritarianism, religious Conservatism and Socio centric attitudes in Roman Catholic groups. Human relations, 1965, 18(3), 231 – 239.
43. Woods J.H., Winger G (1995) Current benzodia zepine issues, Pshycho pharmacology 118(2): 107-15.
44. Abu - Sunhee (1997) DAI-A 58/11, Utah State University p.4181.
45. Aggarwal .J.C. (1986) "*History and Philosophy of Nursery Education*" Douba House, Delhi.
46. Alexander Bay (1990), "*Indian Educational Review*" Fifth Survey P.1235, Vo1.24(1) 84-89.
47. Arora Reela (1998), Fifth Survey Vol,2, p.1860.
48. Avramides Busila (1986), The effect of counseling style on abstracts. New York University. International Vol-47. No.12.
49. Baker, B.L. (1981), Clark .D.B and Yasu Ja P.M, "*Predictors of Success in Parent training*"
50. Barbarasch, Barry Stuart (1997) DAI-A5R/03, Temple University p.74R
51. Berkman .L.F, and Syma .S.L (1979), "*Social Networks, host resistance and morality*", PP.186 - 204.
52. Bigelow, B.J., (1992), The Social Rules that Children Use International Journal of Behavioral Development, V.15, No.3, p.35-36.
53. Bullock J.R. (1993), Children's Loneliness and Their Relationships with Family and Peers, Family Relation, V.42, No.1, p.46-49.
54. Chandy Sumi (1991), Fifth Survey of Research in Education, p.1865..
55. Charlson, E. (1992), How Successful Deaf Teenagers Experience and Cope with Isolation American, Annals of the Deaf, V.137, No.3, p.61-70.
56. Chaube S.P. and Chaube .A. (1999) "*Foundation of education*". Vikas publishing House Pvt.Ltd, New Delhi. p.2SI.
57. Deb Madhu Grewal, Hidraipal (1990), Fifth Survey of Research in Education, p.1868.
58. Derbush, Sanford .M et al, (1991), American Journal of Education Vo1.99, 114p. 543¬
59. Dishion T.J. (1996), preventive parenting with love, Encouragement, and Limit Castalia Publishing Company, P.O. Box 1587.

60. Doctor Z.N (1984), "*Classroom climate and the psyche of pupils and their Achievement*". Further survey of their Research in Edu7cation, Vol. 1, p.821.
61. Dube .A.R. (1989), *"Academic Attainment and Moral of Students taught by teachers using direct and Indirect Influence".* Fifth Survey of Research in Education, p.1878.
62. Estermen, K.(1995), Comparing Rural Adolescents from Farm and Non-farm Families. Journal of Research in Rural Education (V11No.2, p.84-91.
63. Frecknaii P. (1992), An Evaluation of Parental Assessment of the Big Brothers/ Big Sisters Programme in New York City, Adolescence, V.27, N.107, p.15-18.
64. Ganeuly, Malabika (1989), "*Indian Educational Review*" Fifth Survey, P, 1860 , V 0124 (!) p, 84-89.
65. Garison (1992) "*An evaluation of the academic achievement of gifted students from high and low achieving schools 1991*". Boston University. Dissertation Abstracts
66. Giordrane R. (1993), The Family and Peer Relation of Block Adolescents, Journal of Marriage and the Family, V.55, N.2, p.77-87
67. Gnanaraj .J. Gnanadayam (1968) *"Educational Sociology"* p.52.
68. Gomathi Mani (1991) *"Education in the International context."*
69. Hoffmann J.P. (1994), Investigation the Age Effects fo Family Structure Adolecent Marijuana Use, Journal of Youth and Adolescence, V.23, No.2, p.21-35.
70. Hunag Shwu Yung (1995), Effects of Home and School learning environment on the academic achievement of eight grade Asian American Students." International Vol.82.
71. Jack Nobbs, Robert Hine, Margaret E. Fleming (1975) "*Sociology*", MacMillan Education, London;p.44.
72. Jain Shikha (1991) Fifth Survey, p 1879.
73. Jain Shikha (1991), Fifth Survey of Research in Education..P.1879.
74. Janie .E. William (1990), ."*Modeling tests anxiety, Self concept and high school students. Academic Achievement 1990* ", Journal of Research and development in Educational Vo125, 1991 Athens, Georgia
75. Kamala Bhata and Balder Bhatia (1974), "*The Philosophical and Sociological foundations of education*". Doaba House, Delhi .P.102-115.

76. Kimball Yound, Raymond .W. Mack (1959). *"Sociology and Social life."* American, book company, Newyork United States of America. P.348.
77. Levit, M. J, (1995), The Social Convoys of Children and Adolescents.
78. Macires R.M and Charles H.Perge (1971), "*Society: An Introductions Analysis"* Mac Millan. London Press.
79. Meaffee, Mary Elizabeth (1997) DAI-A58/ of from their voices, American Indian in higher education and the phenomenon stepping at (Dropout Persistence) p.2039.
80. Meccarthey, Florence (1997) DAI-A 58/08, Women Instructions in higher education in
81. Milstein, Lindo (1997), AAI-A, 57/12, Family relationship when women and men return to college Adult Students.p.50.
82. Niebrzydowski L. (1995), Adolescents Family Situation and Their Self-Disclosure in Interpersonal Relationship
83. Pardhan .C. (1992). *"Effect of school Organisational Climate on the Creativity, adjustment and academic achievement of Secondary Schools of Orisa"* Educational Vtkal University. Fifth Survey ofTSRE by Buch.
84. Part D. (1993) Fostering Seen by the Careris Children, Adoption Fostering, V.17, p.26-31.
85. Radhi.J (1989) "Home environment Parent child relationship and children's competence during adolescence. p.1018
86. Rahela S.P., Vyas K.C, Dhanpat Rai and Son. *"Sociological Foundations of Education in contemporary India"* p.145.
87. Ram Nath Sharma (1975) *"Introductory Sociology"*, Rajhans Prakashan Mandir, Educational Publishers, Meerut, UP P.250-255.
88. Richard T. Schaefer (1989) *"Sociology"*. Third Edition, M.C. Graw - Hill, Inc. Newyork. p.319.
89. Shukla; Kiran (1992), *"A stud oj development oj social competence as a Junction of parental, behaviour and free interaction"*. Sci - Ravishankar University p.l 024.
90. Shulman S. (1993), Close Relationship and Coping Behaviour in Adolescence, Journal of Adolescence, V.16, No.3, p.67-83.
91. Smith D. (1994), Relationship between Jamaican Adolescent Drinking Partenrs and Self-Image Adolescence, V.28, No.114, p.29-37.
92. Smith MuClialle'J (1995): Dissertation Abstract International Vol.56, No.9.

93. Thapliyal D.P (1981), *"A Study of Classroom Morale, its factors and Relationship with students Academic Achievement"*. Third Survey of Research n Education, by .M.B. Butch.

94. Tolliver and Joel (1995), Dissertation Abstract International Volo.56., No.9.

95. Undheim et aI, (1995), *"Academic achievements of High Ability Students in Egalitarian Education"* The Scandinavian Journal of Educational Research. Vo1.39, n2 p.157- 167.

96. Verma B.P. (1992), Relationshipss between temperament Academic achievement Indian Educational Review" Vo1.27(3). P 95-101

97. Watts, W, (1992), Drug Abuse and Eating Disorders, Journal of Drug Education, V.22, No.3, p.23-40.

98. Webre E. C. (1994), Enhance Social Skills with Peer Recommended Books, Day-Care & Early – Education, V.21, No.4, p.20-24

99 Whister Josue (1992), *"Mid- continent Regional educational lab"*, Aurova, 1992

100. Windle M. (1992), A Longitudinal Study of Stress Buffering for Adolescent Problem Behaviours Developmental Psychology, V.28, No.3, p.522.

102. Youngblade L. M. (1992), Parent Child Antecedent of 5 years old Close Friendship: A Longitudinal Analysis, Developmental Psychology, V.28, N.4, p.7-13.

103. Beck, J. Gayle; McNiff, Judiann; Clapp, Joshua D.; Olsen, Shira A.; Avery, Carlo, Gustavo; McGinley,Meredith; Davis, Alexandra; Streit, CaraChow, Pizza Ka-Yee; Cheng, Sheung-Tak Journal of Counseling Psychology,v57n1 p. 92-104 Jan 2010 and Purpose. Islam&Science, 1(1).

104. De Hoyos, Librado R.; Ramirez, Noe Journal of Ethnic & Cultural Diversity in Social Work, v15 n1-2 p.147-166 2006http://www.tandf.co.uk/journals

105. Diener, E., Emmons, R.A., Larson, R.J., & Griffin, S. (1985). The satisfaction with life scale. Journal of Personality Assessment, 49, 71-75.

106. Dordrecht, Netherlands: Springer, 2005. Phenomenology of Life: Meating the Challanges of the Present Day World (Analecta Husserliana: The Year Book of Phenomenological Research. Vol. LXXXIV)

107. Efthim, Paul W.; Kenny, Maureen E.; Mahalik, James R. Journal of Counselling & Development, v79 n4 p. 30-38 Fall 2001

108. Faiver, Christopher M.; O'Brien, Eugene M.; Ingersoll, R. Elliott Journal of Counselling & Development, v78 n2 p.55-61 Sep 2000

109. Ferguson, Tamara J.; Stegge, Hedy; Miller, Erin R.; Olsen, Michael E. Developmental Psychology, v35 n2 p.47-57 Mar 1999
110. Golshani, Mehdi, 2003. Does Science Offer Evidence of a Transcendent Reality?
111. Grünberg, David, (A) *"The Meaning of Life Vis-A-Vis the Challenges of the Present Day World,"* in Anna-Teresa Tymieniecka (ed.),
112. Grünberg, David, (B) 2005. Etik ve Ya"amın Anlamı, Erdem, 44.
113. Guastello, Stephen, Chaos, Catastrophe, and Human Affairs: Applications of Nonlinear Dynamics to Work, Organizations, and Social Evolution, Lawrence Erlbaum Associates, Mahwah, NJ, 1995.
114. Hesse, Herman, Siddartha, New Directions Paper Book, 1957
115. Hursthouse, Rosalind, 2003, "*Virtue Ethics*", Stanford Encyclopaedia of Philosophy, Edward N. Zalta (ed.), retrieved 6 April, 2010 from http://plato.stanford.edu/entries/ethics-virtue/#2
116. Johnson, Diane Elizabeth College Student Journal, v46 n1 p.3-17 Mar 2012
117. Johnson,Veronica R.F.;Yarhouse, Mark A. Counselling and Values, v58 n1 p.85-103 Apr 2013
118. Joske, W., D. (2004).Philosophy and the Meaning of Life. In David Benatar (ed.), Life, Death and Meaning: Key Philosophical Readings on the Big Questions (pp. 49 – 62). USA, Rowman and Littlefield Publishers Inc. Kraut, Richard, (2001). "Aristotle's Ethics", Stanford Encyclopedia of Philosophy. Retrived August 01, 2010.
118. Kamper, Heidrun Journal of Multilingual and Multicultural Development, v25 n5-6 p.497-511, 2004
119. Kamper, Heidrun Journal of Multilingual and Multicultural Development, v25 n5-6 p.497-511, 2004http://www.tandf.co.uk/journals
120. Kim, Jungmeen; Talbot, Nancy L.; Cicchetti, Dante Child Abuse & Neglect: the International Journal, v33 n6 p.362-371 Jun 2009
121. Kim, Sangmoon; Thibodeau, Ryan; Jorgensen, Randall S. Psychological Bulletin, vo1.37 n1 p.68-96 Jan 2011
122. Kim, Sangmoon; Thibodeau, Ryan; Jorgensen, Randall S. Psychological Bulletin, v137 n1 p.68-96 Jan 2011
123. Kolves, Kairi; Ide, Naoko; De Leo, Diego Suicide and Life-Threatening Behavior, v41 n2 p.149-159 Apr 2011
124. Konstam, Varda; Chernoff, Miriam; Deveney, Sara Counselling and Values, v46 n1 p.26-39 Oct 2001

125. Kristin; Rhea, Deborah J.; Oomen, Jody American Journal of Health Education, v35 n3 p.152-157 May-Jun 2004http://www.aahperd.org
126. Luby, Joan; Belden, Andy; Sullivan, Jill; Hayen, Robin; McCadney, Amber; Spitznagel, Ed Journal of Child Psychology and Psychiatry, v50 n9 p.1156-1166, Sep 2009
127. Megan L.; Hagewood, J. Houston Behavior Therapy, v42 n4 p740-750, Dec 2011
128. Meyer, Janet R. Western Journal of Communication, v77 n2 p.210-230, 2013
129. Mills, R.S.L. Developmental Review, v25 n1 p.26-63, Mar 2005
130. New Directions for Youth Development, n136 p.75-93,2012
131. Thomaes, Sander; Stegge, Hedy; Olthof, Tjeert British Journal of Developmental Psychology, v25 n4 p.559-577, Nov 2007
132. Updike, Thomas L., Jr.; And Others Psychology: A Quarterly Journal of Human Behavior, v24 n1-2 p.60-64, 1987
133. Wietzker, Anne; Buysse, Ann Psychological Assessment, v24 n3 p.783-789, Sep 2012
134. Wiginton, Kristin; Rhea, Deborah J.; Oomen, Jody American Journal of Health Education, v35 n3 p.152-157 May-Jun 2004
135. Wiginton, Kristin; Rhea, Deborah J.; Oomen, Jody American Journal of Health Education, v35 n3 p.152-157 May-Jun 2004
136. Williams, Kate; Donaghue, Ngaire; Kurz, Tim Psychology of Women Quarterly, v37 n1 p.97-112 Mar 2013
137. Williams, Neil F. Journal of Physical Education, Recreation & Dance, v86 n1 p.36-39 2015
138. Wilson, Tom Journal of Education & Christian Belief, v18 n2 p.155-169, 2014

❑❑❑